BREAKING CONTRACT

The Story of Vinnia Ndadi

Recorded and edited by Dennis Mercer

BREAKING CONTRACT

The Story of Vinnia Ndadi

Recorded and edited by Dennis Mercer

IDAF PUBLICATIONS LTD.
A publishing company of
International Defence and Aid Fund for Southern Africa
1989

© IDAF PUBLICATIONS LTD.

First published by LSM Press, Canada 1974
Published by IDAF Publications Ltd. 1989

ISBN 0904759 98 3 (Hardback)
ISBN 0904759 96 9 (Paperback)

The International Defence and Aid Fund for Southern Africa is a humanitarian organisation which has worked consistently for peaceful and constructive solutions to the problems created by racial oppression in Southern Africa.

It sprang from Christian and humanist opposition to the evils and injustices of apartheid in Southern Africa. It is dedicated to the achievement of free, democratic, non-racial societies throughout Southern Africa.

The objects of the Fund are:

(i) to aid, defend and rehabilitate the victims of unjust legislation and oppressive and arbitrary procedures,

(ii) to support their families and dependants,

(iii) to keep the conscience of the world alive to the issues at stake.

In accordance with these three objects, the Fund distributes its humanitarian aid to the victims of racial injustice without any discrimination on grounds of race, colour, religious or political affiliation. The only criterion is that of genuine need.

The Fund runs a comprehensive information service on affairs in Southern Africa; this includes visual documentation. The Fund prides itself on the strict accuracy of all its information. Associated with IDAF is a publishing company IDAF Publications Ltd. which produces a regular news bulletin *FOCUS on Political Repression in Southern Africa*. It also publishes pamphlets and books and produces films and photographic exhibitions on all aspects of repression and resistance in Southern Africa.

The IDAF Publications Ltd. reprint series consists of writings from an earlier period of the history of the struggle against apartheid and minority rule in Southern Africa, writings which have gone out of print but which the Fund believes have relevance today.

No attempt has been made to verify details, and they are presented as products of their own time and circumstances. Inevitably they would have been written differently in certain respects had the authors been writing today. They may contain material which with hindsight and in the light of advances in historical knowledge would have been differently stated. The views and interpretations they express are not necessarily those of the Fund.

They are reprinted as historical documents in the belief that their availability will widen understanding of the struggle for freedom in Southern Africa and of the issues at stake.

Printed by Honey Press Ltd, Banbury

Contents

NAMIBIA

- ■● MAJOR TOWNS
- ○ OTHER TOWNS
- —— MAJOR ROADS
- ++++ RAILWAYS
- ⌒ PERENNIAL RIVERS

0   200

KILOMETRES

Preface

Breaking Contract gives a unique insight into the conditions, events and personalities which gave rise to the formation of the South West African People's Organisation, SWAPO of Namibia, and the launching of its armed struggle for freedom from South Africa.

The book takes its name from the system of migrant contract labour which had a profound effect on the lives of Namibians and shaped resistance to South African rule.

The life story of Helao Vinnia Ndadi, as recorded and edited by Dennis Mercer, *Breaking Contract* was first published by LSM Press in Canada in 1974. It documents, in Ndadi's own words, his experiences as a contract worker under apartheid and his role in organising the Ovamboland People's Organisation, which in 1960 became SWAPO.

Minor changes and corrections have been made to this edition, mostly in the spelling of names which have been updated to follow current Namibian orthography. The original foreword and introduction have been replaced, and Ndadi has written a new postscript.

PART ONE

Contract worker

1 Men in cattle cars

My name is Vinnia Ndadi. I was born at Ouhongo village in Ovamboland on 14 October 1928. I was the second child in my family, following my brother Jackson, or Hamutenya as we called him. Later I had two more brothers and a sister. Our family owned a plot of land which my father and mother worked.

My parents came to Ouhongo from Okafima, now part of Angola, in 1917 when the Portuguese invaded the Kingdom of Mandume. King Mandume fled to Ondjiva where a fierce battle with the Portuguese ensued. Mandume, badly wounded and out of ammunition, shot himself rather than be killed by his enemies. The Portuguese then set out to kill all his relatives — with the help of the South Africans, who were acting on the orders of the British. My father was related to the king. He is from the Ovakwaanime or Lion clan, very respected and important in the Oukwanyama tribe. So, when the Portuguese moved in he left to settle in Namibia, at Ouhongo.

Though popular and respected because of his clan, my father made many enemies when he became a Christian. Usually people would help a young man get started in life, giving him four or five cows, for example, when he got married. But this was not the case with my father. He had to rely on himself.

At Ouhongo my father planted *omahangu*, a small grain which my mother ground into a wonderful white meal and boiled it until it was thick. This *oshifima*, as we called it, was then eaten with meat, or if meat wasn't available, we had a thinner porridge with milk. We also grew vegetables — pumpkins, beans, ground-nuts, monkey-nuts, cabbage, beets, and so forth.

My parents worked together in the fields except when my father was away working on contract. He was gone quite a lot and my mother then took over the responsibilities of the kraal, or homestead.

11

In those days everyone used hoes to work the land — ploughs being introduced at Ouhongo only much later.

In addition to work in the fields my mother looked after the house and children, preparing our meals, drawing water and so on. Water was always a problem at Ouhongo. Though I never experienced drought or famine myself, I remember my parents and the older people always talking about times when there was no rain and many people died of hunger. We had a small well near our kraal, dug by my father, but it never yielded enough water. Every day the women walked seven miles with buckets and gourds to get water.

While still very young I played at home and helped my mother with small tasks. When I was five I began helping in the fields and looking after our cattle. Like the other children not in school, I often went gathering wild fruit. During the rainy season, January to May, the tall *omive* tree bore a fruit called *eembe* which fell to the ground after heavy rains. We collected the *eembe* in baskets, then washed and dried them for storing. Another job I had during the rainy season was to chase birds from our crops. My brother and I would shout 'Whoo-whoo-whoo!' and scare the birds away.

During the dry season there wasn't much to do. The vegetables and most of the fruit had already been dried and stored. In winter I had small chores like collecting firewood, tending new-born lambs and kids, and helping my parents harvest the *matio* and *omiandi* trees.

Ouhongo is a very beautiful area, especially when the trees grow their new leaves. I always enjoyed going to the bush to collect fruit and hunt with my friends. I also liked taking our cattle to graze a few miles away from the village. During the rainy season the pastures were swampy, but when they dried the grass grew tall and green.

Ouhongo had sixteen kraals, covering about fifty square kilometres. In Angola kraals hold about ten families, but in Oukwanyama they are much smaller. Our kraal had separate huts for my parents, me and my brothers and later my sister. Another hut, the *epata*, was used only for preparing meals. In addition we had huts for three Angolans who stayed with us for four years.

Angolans often came to Ouhongo to exchange things like tobacco for cattle or goats. First they would find a person to stay with, then people would come to buy their things. Some traders were not accepted because they didn't know anybody to keep them or recommend them to headmen. The fellows at our kraal were practically citizens of Ouhongo by the time they returned to Angola.

My father was master of our kraal and responsible for keeping it up. Our huts, made of wood with mud-packed walls and grass roofs, were surrounded by a strong, high wood and thorn fence. My father also fenced our fields and maintained a separate kraal for our livestock. This was to protect the animals and also to keep them out of our crops. I think people first made kraals for protection against dangerous animals like lions and leopards.

Each kraal was run by a family head, like my father; but there was also a headman, responsible for maintaining the traditional laws of the whole village. When somebody broke a law, the people offended would bring the matter to the headman. I remember one case when a boy in the village caused a young girl to become pregnant. This was a serious offence and according to old laws the boy would have been killed. Now, however, it was handled differently. The headman fined the boy two cattle, one for violating the girl's virginity and the other for the baby. 'The laws of Oukwanyama have changed,' my father told me, 'because of the Church. People now believe in the commandment, "Thou shall not kill."'

My parents were both Christians, so in addition to the stories I heard about our old traditions I also learned about Christianity.

When I was about eight I started Standard 1 at the Finnish Missionary School at Engela. Before that I went to introductory school at Ouhongo for a year. It was for pre-Standard 1; there was only one teacher, who taught us a little reading and writing. I was happy to be starting the mission school but sad that most of my friends — whose parents weren't Christians — wouldn't be joining me. Engela was the only school in our area and it was reserved for children of Christian parents.

I had visited Engela before. When still a little boy I had *evambala*, a stomach sickness, and had to be carried the seven miles to Engela hospital. Later I went there with a swollen foot. I hated the hospital at first, but after a few times I got used to it. In fact, I even thought about becoming a doctor some day.

Like the school, Engela hospital was run by Finnish missionaries assisted by Africans. Few missionaries knew our language or way of life very well; nor did they understand or respect traditional medicines. A few people died from modern medicines after they had been getting traditional treatment.

My aunt was one of our own doctors; she could cure many sicknesses, including snake bites. We had poisonous snakes like black and brown mambas and insects, whose poison would kill you in less than five hours. During the rainy season mosquitoes from flooded areas brought malaria to the village, and people often got sick from eating green vegetables and *eembe*. To cure these things my aunt used herbs and traditional prayers.

I went to the mission school for seven years. We had about 500 students — mostly boys — and six or seven teachers. Each grade was divided into two classes of about forty students each which usually shared one teacher. My teacher in Standard 1 was Joseph Hangula, who had gone to the Finnish Missionary Teachers' Training School at Oniipa, in the Ondangua area. I can see now that my teachers were not well educated themselves, but they did help us learn a few things, like Arithmetic, European History and Geography — at least where Africa was. My favourite subjects were Geography, Afrikaans and especially Nature Studies. Each year I passed a Standard (though I had to repeat Standard 4) until I completed Standard 6 in 1943. That year my teacher was Paulus Nakale, later appointed Inspector of the Ovamboland Schools when 'Bantu Education' was introduced in 1955 by the South African government.

There was no secondary school in our area and my parents couldn't afford to send me to boarding school. So, the only thing I could do after finishing Standard 6 was to stay at home and help my parents.

I had liked school very much — though I couldn't understand all the subjects very well. As I recall, Afrikaans was introduced at Engela in 1939. It was something very new for us, this foreign language; we spoke only Oshikwanyama before. English wasn't taught but I picked up a few words from my father who'd learned a bit when he worked as a docker at Walvis Bay in 1905–7 when it was occupied by the British. He would sometimes say 'Good morning' or 'How are you?' And I would answer 'OK', or 'Fine'.

The most difficult thing about school was getting there, especially when the weather was bad. Every day I had to walk fourteen miles.

I got up at 7 a.m., had some *oshikundu* — our usual millet porridge — and set off with some friends. Classes started at 11 — they couldn't begin any earlier because many children came from as far as fifteen miles away — from Ohaingu area, for instance. Almost every day we had to run part of the way, afraid of being punished if we came late.

Most of us didn't have shoes or warm clothing. I remember in winter my feet usually got very sore and cut — and a few times I became sick from the cold. When my father was working on contract he didn't have enough money to buy us good clothes. He worked for five or six shillings a month; barely enough for bread, much less clothes or cattle or things for the kraal. Some children at Engela were from rich families and had warm clothes and shoes. We poor kids could not enjoy seeing some students wearing nice things while we were in rags.

At school I couldn't concentrate on my lessons very well — mostly because I was always hungry and tired. I didn't bring bread or anything else for lunch and at school we got nothing — not even tea. So we just got used to going hungry until classes were over at 5 and we could get home for supper. If I was detained for coming late in the morning, then I would have to run home to get my chores done before eating. I always had chores; it was never just coming home and finding dinner ready to eat. I had to bring in the cattle, fetch some wood, and so on. After supper I did my school assignments with friends. We didn't have money to buy the texts, so I went to a friend's and we would study together. Sometimes I would borrow his book overnight. I think this is how my schooling suffered most; I was always having to borrow books or to do without.

Discipline at school was strict. If caught sleeping in class, you had to stand for thirty minutes in a corner. In handicrafts we made baskets, mats, sun hats. If you worked slowly and carefully they accused you of being lazy, making you sweep up the classroom every day for a week. If you were late for class you had to stay after school for an hour or so and walk (usually run) home alone.

In the afternoons we sometimes played games. We boys usually tied together rags and used it for a football. Girls had their own games. For example, they tied palm leaves together to make jump ropes. Most of the time, though, we were in class.

15

I had some good friends at Engela school but most lived far away. When at home I played with my Ouhongo friends. Sometimes we went hunting, or played football. Some of these old friends are still there today, but most have died.

Phillip was one of my best friends. He died in 1957. His house was not far from ours, so we always walked to school together. One day on our way to school a man with a dog approached us. His dog barked and charged at us. I grabbed a stick and hit it. The man got very angry and began to beat us. I said, 'If you don't stop, we'll have to fight. We won't just let you beat us!' So we began to fight. Every boy had to know how to fight with a *knobkierie* (stick), where to hit and how to defend himself. But this man was stronger than both of us together and he even broke Phillip's stick. So we ran off and kept running all the way to school as we were already late.

Another friend of mine was a very good swimmer. I couldn't swim very well but, anyway, one day we decided to swim across the river. I got to the middle and then started having trouble. 'Help!' I yelled. 'I'm going down!' He just laughed,'Yeah, I can see! There you go . . .' When he finally realised I was really in trouble he came over and pulled me to the bank.

When I finished Standard 6, my father was away in the army. It was during World War II. I couldn't continue at another school, as I said, because I was needed for work at home and we couldn't afford the boarding fees. Still today, this hasn't changed — if you want a child well educated in Namibia, it costs a lot of money.

My father came home in 1944, after more than three years in the army. He had been getting a small salary, which he sent to my mother at the Oshikango Administrative Centre. It wasn't much; two pounds, sometimes one pound ten. But my mother saved it and when my father returned he was able to buy some things for the kraal — corn, a few cows, more goats, etc. He never received any military compensation — that was only for Whites! Even poor Whites became rich after the war when they were given free land.

For the next several years, I helped work the family land at Ouhongo. My younger brothers Alexander and Issaschar, and my sister Hilalia, went to school during this time — but they also helped out at the kraal. Growing crops is not an easy thing. We worked the soil with hoes, then planted — mostly *omahangu*, because it can resist drought for over a month, and also maize. Beans are also strong, but many other vegetables, like pumpkins, would die when there was little rain.

Harvesting was done by hand. *Omahangu*, for example, was plucked off the stalks like maize, then pounded to force the grain out of the shell. To get these grains out cleanly you tossed the pounded *omahangu* up in the air from a basket so that the grain fell back while the shells were blown away by the wind. This, of course, is the old method of winnowing we used to separate the millet or other grains from the chaff and dirt.

By the time I left Ouhongo in 1946 some changes had taken place. More children were now at school, as Christians increased or more people began to see the value of education. Then in 1947 some people began to buy ploughs. Those without cattle used donkeys to pull their ploughs, and in a few years just about everyone was ploughing their land instead of hoeing. This meant they could grow more crops and be sure of having enough to eat during the dry season.

I was very young — still seventeen in fact — when I first went to SWANLA (South West Africa Native Labour Association), the central recruiting agency for contract labour, in 1946. I wanted to continue school, but had instead to think of work. One day I walked to the SWANLA recruiting station in Ondangua. They laughed and sent me back saying I was too young and weak. Employers buying people from SWANLA wanted strong boys able to do hard work in mines and on farms, not young boys unable to lift even a bag of cement. I was sent back like this four times before they finally accepted me. I really wanted to go. There was nothing else; no schooling, just work on the land.

Once accepted I was examined and classified as a 'Grade C boy'. Workers were — and still are — classified according to their health; the strength of their bodies. That's the only important thing to the recruiting agent — he doesn't want to buy a sick or weak person unable to perform the work he is contracted for. At Ondangua, after our physical examinations (they treated us like cattle) they graded the very strong and healthy ones as 'A' boys; those with good health but not so strong as 'B' boys; and the youngest and weakest as 'C' boys. The wage for those of us classed as 'C' was eight shillings a

17

month. For 'A' boys it was fifteen shillings and 'B' boys got ten. After my physical examination I was tagged with a number and my 'C' classification. I had to wear this tag on a string around my neck.

Later that day all of us who passed were put into buses and taken to the SWANLA camp just outside Grootfontein. As soon as we got there we were formed into a long line while a man counted up the 'A', 'B' and 'C' boys. Then we went to the big compound and joined all the others who were waiting for their papers and transport south.

I soon learned that how long you stayed at the SWANLA camp depended on when your *baas* (boss or employer) sent the money for your transportation. If he didn't send this money with his original order for workers, you could wait as along as a month. I was lucky my first time; I waited less than a week.

The camp at Grootfontein consisted of SWANLA offices and barracks for the contract workers, surrounded by a high, barbed wire fence. The workers' barracks were called *pondoks*. They had zinc roofs, concrete floors and no beds — each man just got two dirty, lice-infested blankets to sleep on. The place was filthy and hot — with lots of bugs; big ones. The smell was so bad I couldn't sleep for several hours that first night. We had just one bucket for twenty people and I usually preferred to go out into the bush to relieve myself. The food was terrible also — just mealie meal and a small piece of meat once a week. They had new recruits mix the dough for bread with their feet. It was horrible — stale and usually mouldy.

Finally they assigned you a job: 'Johannes! You're going to milk cows on the "X" Farm'; 'Samuel! You'll work at the Tsumeb mines!' And so on. You couldn't refuse. At first I said to myself that I wouldn't just take any job, but when I saw a man badly beaten for refusing his 'contract', I decided to take whatever they gave me. Fortunately, I was told, 'Vinnia — you'll work as a "houseboy" for a Mr Jooste. He's a farmer in the Mariental District.'

I went by train from Grootfontein to Mariental, in the south. It was a small train that we called '*kataula*' (cutting through) because it went so fast. We squeezed into small cattle cars, more than twenty men in each. They put canvas down to cover the cattle mess but it was impossible to lie down. I stood or sat the whole five days to Mariental. There were no buckets or latrines. We just had to wait each time till the next station — if we could — then run to the bush or latrine. Also there was no water on the *kataula*; cattle could survive without it for days. Eating dry bread I got extremely thirsty, which was worse than the hunger.

There were a few good coaches on this train reserved for Whites or for Blacks or Coloureds living within the 'Police Zone'. As 'contract labourers' from native reserves we were kept separate. One day we crossed the 'red line' into the area of white settlement — a Police Zone running from Tsumeb all the way to the Orange River border with South Africa.

At Mariental station I was told to wait till my boss came for me. I stayed in a station *pondok* till Mr Jooste arrived a week later. He was surprised to find I could speak a little Afrikaans. He said, 'Besides being my "houseboy", you can translate for me with the other workers.' Jooste was a very rich Boer with many Ovambos working on his farm.

Before we left the station, Jooste went to a hotel in the town for something to eat. 'Are you hungry?' he asked. 'Well, yes *baas*, a bit,' I replied. When we reached some hotel he told a kitchen worker to get me some food. I sat outside and finally the man brought some food and coffee in a tin. I gulped it down immediately. After three weeks on a SWANLA diet I was literally starving.

Jooste's farm was bigger than any I'd ever seen. Surrounded by tall trees were fields of potatoes, cabbage, carrots and other vegetables, as well as orchards of fruit like grapes and figs. Jooste sold his crops in town — to hotels, schools, etc. He also had plenty of grazing land, mostly for sheep.

There were eleven other Ovambos working at the farm. Some tended herds, others milked the cows or worked the fields. Every morning at 5 a big bell rang to wake us up. We had to be at work by 6. In the dry season the shepherds got up even earlier to take the sheep to good pastures and water far away.

My first job in the morning was making coffee for the *baas* and the *missus* — as we were forced to call them. Then I prepared meals, cleaned the house — sweeping, dusting, washing the floors, etc. — chopped wood, watered the flowers and did odd jobs around the house.

Field workers quit at 5 and shepherds came back around 6; but I usually worked till 10 p.m. or later. When visitors came I served food and drinks, then washed the dishes and cleaned up after they left.

Saturdays I counted sheep, keeping a weekly record book because the *baas* was always worried about losing sheep. I remember one shepherd, Johannes, who looked after forty sheep. One day a sheep strayed and was eaten by jackals. The *baas* was very angry, shouting that he would beat Johannes. Johannes wasn't afraid; Jooste was seventy-two and an *oubaas* who couldn't do much beating. So Johannes just looked up at the sky, not even seeming to listen.

Next day Jooste's two sons arrived. They had farms close by. Johannes was in the *pondok*. They called him. '*Baas*?' 'Come here!' I was asked to translate. 'The *oubaas* told us he won't stand for any more of your arrogant nonsense. You're not looking after his sheep well, so he's going to beat you.' Johannes was furious and I indicated this in my translation: 'You just tell the *baas* that if he tries to beat me I'll resist.' The two sons moved in fast and grabbed Johannes, throwing him to the ground and starting to hit and hit him. Somehow, Johannes managed to break loose and start running. They chased him a long way but finally gave up. The *oubaas* was just bent over laughing at the sight of the chase. Next morning Johannes came back. The old *baas* just said 'Jo, you'd better be more careful with my sheep!'

It wasn't long, however, before Johannes lost another sheep. The *oubaas* again called in his boys and this time they seized the shepherd and dragged him into the *waenhuis*, a big barn where they keep cars, equipment, supplies and so on. They threw him over a bag of salt and held him there. One man held Jo's arms, the other his legs and Jooste whipped him hard with a piece of rope, just whipped him till he was satisfied or too tired to go on. Then Johannes got up and ran away. But the next day he came back; there was no place else for him to go.

Being interpreter was a very bad job. I said what the Boer told me to, but sometimes the workers thought I was on his side. And if I didn't translate correctly, the *baas* would say, 'What's wrong? Don't they understand? Tell them exactly what I said!' And sometimes, when I didn't tell the *baas* exactly what a worker said (because I knew the fellow would be beaten for it) then the man got angry and even threatened me. It was very difficult work.

I remember once when it was really dry and grazing was very poor. Sheep ran after every little thing to eat. One fellow got into trouble for losing part of his flock. Threatened with a beating, he said, 'I won't be beaten — instead I'll beat up the *baas!*' I couldn't say this to the *oubaas*. I was silent for a moment . . . but the man insisted; 'Tell him what I said.' 'Well,' I told the *baas*, 'Hamakali has said that if you try and beat him, he'll beat you instead.' Jooste's face got red. 'So, you want to beat up the *oubaas*, eh, Hamakali? Is that true?' 'Yes,' replied Hamakali. 'Well, we'll just see. If you don't straighten up by tomorrow, we'll take you to Mariental where the police will deal with your case.'

Hamakali just stood there — refusing to return to work. The *oubaas* had him tied up and taken straight to the police. Inside the station they beat him severely . . . didn't even ask what happened. Their job is to remind contract labourers that they're working for the *oubaas* and have to be respectful and obedient.

Still, old Jooste wasn't as bad as most. White farmers could get away with anything . . . treat their workers just as they pleased. Many times we heard about men being shot dead by their *baas* just for talking back. The law did nothing, of course — it was made for the Whites! We couldn't resist or even complain without being beaten or sent back to Ovamboland with no pay. We had to learn to survive; to keep quiet and finish our contracts.

After three years at the Jooste farm I was weak and tired. Three years of nothing but maize meal porridge, a little salt, and occasional meat when a diseased sheep died. I prepared *oshifima* twice a day, but the shepherds ate only in the evening. We seldom had breakfast and were so exhausted from the work that we slept like dead men. By the time my contract expired in 1950 I was very excited about going home.

I left, tired of the farm and without much money. The *oubaas* drove me to the railway station where I waited for a week for my train. I stayed in one of the two station *pondoks*, sleeping in my blankets on the dirt floor together with five other contract workers returning home.

The only food was mealie meal that we got from the station storeroom and prepared ourselves. Firewood was very scarce, so some mornings I'd get up early and walk fifteen miles to the bush.

People in the location — the African quarter outside the city — had used up the nearby wood. The first day I walked for two hours and couldn't even find one stick on the ground. I finally had to climb a tree to get some dead branches near the top. Then I started going to the more distant bush. Usually I bundled and carried more than I needed, selling some in the location. It was common practice for contract workers waiting at the station to collect and sell firewood to the local people. Sometimes they stopped me on the path from the forest or even came to the station. I usually got back late — 3 or 4 in the afternoon — and fixed my meal.

In the morning I made porridge with milk; for supper it was the thicker *oshifima*. I got water from a tap at the station and boiled it in a pot over three stones. Then I stirred in the mealie meal until it was good and thick, but with no clots. At home we ate this *oshifima* with meat, but now I could afford only sugar and milk.

After supper I sat down with my friends in the *pondok*. We talked into the night, exchanging stories and experiences — about our contracts, our work, how we were treated by our *baas*, and so forth. Some of these men had been working on a farm called Tugela, about four miles from old Jooste's place. One of them slaughtered a sheep in the bush one day — because the farmer never gave them any meat, just mealie meal and salt. Only the 'houseboy' sometimes got a few odd scraps from the *baas's* table.

This worker at Tugela was caught and beaten by the *baas*. Then he ran away. He was walking to Mariental when he looked around and saw the farm lorry coming after him. He panicked and just started running down the road, not thinking to turn and hide in the bush. The lorry chased him till he couldn't run any more. Driving were the sons of the *oubaas* and these young fellows were even more vicious than the *oubaas*. When the '*klein base*' or 'small bosses', as they are called, finally caught up with him, the man tried to climb a tree but he was so tired he slipped and fell to the ground. They threw him on the truck and took him back to the farm. There they beat him very badly with a long piece of garden hose.

When I met him in the *pondok* he was seriously ill. There was blood in his urine and he had terrible stomach pains. Apparently he was injured internally. Earlier, when he asked the *oubaas* to be taken to hospital, the *baas* refused, saying 'You're lucky I didn't kill you or take you to the police. Just shut up and stop complaining.' I heard many stories like this while waiting at the railway station. With Ovambos I talked about life in Ovamboland, recalling common friends and incidents at home. Most of us had been away a long time. On contract you got no chance to visit your home and family.

People around the station didn't care much for contract labourers, especially farm workers, so we kept mostly to ourselves. There was no chance to be with a woman in Mariental. We had heard what happened if a contract man even tried to talk to a woman. But I didn't care; I was going home where I was better known than in any other place. So I just forgot about other things and waited for my train to Ovamboland.

I left Jooste's farm with less than two pounds . . . after three whole years! Once my father wrote saying the family needed money, so I sent some through the post from Mariental. I also bought a jacket for my father and a few little things for the rest of the family — as well as some trousers for myself. I had just enough money left for the long trip to Ovamboland.

We finally left Mariental station one evening at about 7 o'clock. It was a passenger train this time, divided into first class coaches for Whites, a coach for local people going to Windhoek, and one (third class) for contract labourers. It wasn't nearly as bad as the first train from Grootfontein, when we were put in cattle cars. Now we had bench seats, windows and a little room to walk about. The *oubaas* paid for our ticket; it was in the contract.

Having been in a semi-desert at the farm in eastern Mariental for three years, I really enjoyed seeing the beautiful green mountains and forests as we moved to the north. Coming into Windhoek, too, I saw such a different world . . . so many people, streets and big buildings. I was worried, though. On the train I heard about big floods in the north, around the Namutoni River, which had washed out the road to Ovamboland. Contract workers, people said, were just sitting, waiting in Grootfontein. I thought a while, then decided it was better to wait in Windhoek than in the SWANLA camp at Grootfontein.

When I told my friends I wasn't going on, since the roads to Ondangua were closed by floods, they tried to warn me against staying in Windhoek, saying that without a pass I would be arrested.

'I don't care,' I said, 'let them arrest me; it's still better than waiting around in Grootfontein.' They knew what I meant. We'd all heard stories of workers starving in the SWANLA camp there.

In Windhoek I went to a hotel where I'd learned a friend of mine from Engela school was working as a waiter. It was the Grosshertzog Hotel, an old place run by Germans. My friend, Samuel, was very happy to see me after such a long time. He led me to his room, then went out to get some food. He explained that he was on duty, but when he got off we could talk more.

Later I told him how it was at the farm and asked him about Windhoek. He said it was a very rough place, the police being extremely vicious. 'If you're arrested without a pass, they beat you and leave you to rot in prison. If they find you're a contract labourer, they assume you've broken contract and are just roaming around the city, so, they beat you and send you back to your *baas*.' I made up my mind to be very careful in Windhoek.

The following morning Sam took me out walking, showing me the city. First we went to the main street, Kaiserstrasse — named after the Emperor when Namibia was a German colony. It was very strange seeing all those nice clothes and other things in store windows. Next we went to the location where Sam introduced me to some of his friends. We talked and drank *karie* beer. It's made from green peas, called *ertjies* in Afrikaans, soaked in warm water with *oufila* yeast, sugar and sometimes fruit like pineapple or bananas. Then it's left in a calabash or a bucket to ferment overnight. It tasted good and strong; a little like our beer at Ouhongo — except that ours was corn beer, boiled with honey.

This was the first time I'd drunk *ertjies* beer and I got so drunk I couldn't even walk. Samuel had to return for work but I was staggering so badly he had to help me to the hotel. He put me to bed, then locked the door behind him. Late in the evening he returned. 'Hey, *ou maat*!' (We called each other *ou maat* — 'old friend' in Afrikaans.) 'I'm all right,' I said. Then we talked a bit and went to sleep. Next morning I had a terrible headache. Sam said, 'Man, you've got to take care of yourself. Here, take some aspirin and orange squash.'

Feeling better later, I asked Sam about my chances of getting a job in Windhoek. 'Well, things are tough here,' he said, 'but you can go

24

ahead and try. Go to the Native Affairs Department and tell them why you can't go on to Ovamboland. They just may give you a work permit.'

Being off duty that afternoon, Sam took me there himself. It was 2.30 and they were just reopening after lunch. To my amazement I discovered a friend working right there at the front counter . . . Simon Nehemia, son of our headman at Ouhongo. I told him I'd arrived from Mariental two days earlier and didn't know what to do. 'They told me SWANLA buses couldn't get to Ovamboland because of the floods and that even Namutoni bridge had washed away. There's no reason going to Grootfontein in a situation like that, so I'm looking for a job here — just for a couple of months — until the situation improves up north.' Simon said, 'Well, you may have a chance. I'll talk to the Native Commissioner.' This Commissioner was appointed from South Africa, under its Native Affairs administration. Since Simon was a friend, I knew he'd put my request in the best terms.

In a few minutes he returned and said, 'Well man, I tried hard, but the Commissioner just said, "We'll see. Tell him to come again tomorrow."' I thanked Simon but left with little hope.

I went back the following morning around nine. Simon was a bit surprised. 'Oh, you're back.' 'Yes. You know I'm very serious.' 'OK,' he said, 'I'll go remind the *baas*.' He was gone a long time. But finally he came back smiling. 'Here's your pass, Vinnia! Remember, it's good for two months. Before it expires bring it in and we might get it extended.' I was really happy about the pass, but now I needed a job. 'Well,' Simon said, 'I can't help you there. Just go round to industrial firms like Pupkewitch & Sons or Lewis Construction Co., or to the hotels and restaurants. If you're lucky you'll find something.'

I was just leaving when a white man came in, nicely dressed in a black street suit. His name was Zander. He told Simon he needed some local 'boys' for his cafe. Simon called me aside and whispered. 'Look, this guy is the owner of a big restaurant, the Zoo Cafe. You want a job there?' 'Great,' I said. And it was as simple as that.

We got into Zander's car and drove to the cafe. Inside it was very busy. Waiters were rushing back and forth, the kitchen door kept swinging, and I saw young boys inside feverishly washing dishes and peeling potatoes. These workers were Africans, many from South Africa.

Zander took me into his office and said, 'You will be a waiter. How much pay do you want?' I started to say 'Five pounds a month,' but then hesitated a moment. It seemed so much compared to the eight shillings I was earning on the farm. 'But you never know,' I thought, 'he just might agree.' So I said, 'Well, *oubaas* . . . I would like five pounds.' 'Oh, five pounds, eh?' He paused. 'Well, OK, but you'd better be a nice boy and behave like a real gentleman.'

He called in the head waiter, a man from Malawi, and told him to show me my job, setting tables, serving and so forth. I was given a white uniform and started work immediately. It wasn't hard. The only difficulty was not knowing English or being really fluent in Afrikaans. But my Afrikaans was good enough to wait on tables and talk to Zander, who was a Boer from South Africa. All the customers were White, of course, and most spoke Afrikaans.

I worked without a break until midnight, the closing time. As we were changing out of our uniforms in the back, the head waiter told me I would be working the evening shift, from 4 p.m. till midnight. I did this for a few weeks, but then was put on the day shift, which was less tiring because there weren't so many customers or big parties.

That first night, when we got outside, I realised I didn't know how to get back to the hotel. I asked the head waiter. 'No problem,' he said, 'we use the Zoo car.' So they dropped me off at the hotel. I had to wake Sam up so he could let me in, but he was happy to see me again. 'Where have you been, man? I was afraid you'd been arrested.' We sat and I told him the whole story.

Next day I was washing my clothes when Sam came over and said, 'Vinnia, those shorts are for the farm, man. You're in town now; they don't wear those things here.' He was right. The men I saw in Windhoek all wore nice clothes — long pants, sports jackets, and even suits. But I had nothing but shorts, a cotton shirt called a 'skipper,' and a pair of black shoes I'd bought in Mariental.

'What should I do? I don't have money for such nice clothes.' Sam then went to his closet and took out a pair of trousers, a white shirt and a jacket. 'Here, use these for now. When you start getting paid from your job you'll be able to buy some more and better things.' I put Sam's clothes on and went out for a walk alone. I didn't go far — fearing I'd get lost, but I was already more comfortable in Windhoek than a few days before.

Soon I got used to my job and there was plenty to eat at the Zoo. My problem became where to stay. I shared Sam's room for a couple of weeks, but that was illegal and the hotel staff were becoming very suspicious. One day I met some old friends from home. 'Look,' they said, 'you can't sleep in the streets. Come stay with us.' So the next day I moved in with my friend Absalom. I had to avoid being seen by his *baas*, but it wasn't as risky as at the hotel.

On contract as a domestic servant, Absalom lived in a one-room shack behind his master's house. I stayed there a week — until the *missus* saw me leaving one morning. She spoke to Absalom. 'Who was that Ovambo I saw leaving your house this morning? Has he been sleeping here?' 'No, ma'am! He was just visiting.' Nevertheless, I had to move on again that night.

At the next place I stayed for only five days. My friend's contract expired and he wanted to leave immediately for Ovamboland. I tried to persuade him to stay but he said he was completely fed up with life in Windhoek. 'It's even better waiting around Grootfontein than working for these people,' he said.

It was Sunday and I walked out to the railway compound where I met many old friends. They had heard I was in Windhoek but couldn't get in touch with me. I explained I'd been moving around a lot and why. They said, 'The situation here is very bad. Police come by at night, searching everywhere and arresting anyone found sleeping here illegally. You're welcome to stay but the risk is great.' What could I do? It was like that everywhere, even in town. So we talked and then they showed me some hidden sleeping places in the compound.

The railway compound had twelve *pondoks* for contract workers employed either on the railroad or by the municipality. It was surrounded by a 15-foot-high barbed wire fence and had only one gate, guarded by a watchman. Nobody entered unless he was known to the watchman or produced a pass. If he was stopped and found to be there illegally, he was taken to the compound superintendent and then turned over to the municipal police. Sometimes they also informed the South African Police, Native Affairs police or the railway police — there was no shortage of police in Windhoek! I was lucky — always walking in and out with crowds of friends and never being discovered.

It must be said that the watchmen too were Ovambos and many would never inform on their fellows. A few, though, were stupid; wanting to be in the 'good' with their *baas*, expecting favours or more money. These types, however, were also cowards who feared being beaten up as informers. So it wasn't often that Ovambos were caught and turned in to the police.

Every morning I woke up at 5 and set out with the others, not wanting to risk being seen and questioned by the police. Even while still working the night shift, I left early in the morning and walked to the Zoo, got something to eat, talked with the boys in the kitchen and passed my day writing letters and reading sports magazines from South Africa. I especially enjoyed the boxing magazines.

On the job I worked hard and avoided all trouble with customers, even the worst ones. What could I do anyway? They were White and 'owned' the law and police. Also, I had to be careful as I was there illegally once my permit expired.

I worked at the Zoo for five months. The floods had risen, levelled, then passed. I knew they wouldn't extend my permit after the first two months but wanted to stay because the job paid a high salary plus tips. I was now able to buy nice things for my family and good clothes for myself. At that time I wanted very much to 'fit in' with the well-dressed Windhoek Africans. I remember buying a black pin-striped suit the first chance I got. I was so caught up in this clothes thing that sometimes I even dreamed about it.

Working six days a week, I had little free time and much of that I spent in the compound with my friends. As in Mariental, I had no girlfriends. Ovambo girls in Windhoek, even prostitutes, looked down on contract workers. But I wasn't much interested anyway. While my permit was valid I usually went to the African location on my day off; I passed the time drinking *karie* beer, which I was getting used to, and talking to friends.

The African location is an old, dilapidated place which goes back to the time of German colonization. There are rows and rows of shacks with sagging walls and rusted-out roofs. Over the years people just settled there on government orders and managed to build whatever homes they could. The best type had brick walls with an inside ceiling, zinc roof and small garden. Most, however, were made of wood with leaky tin roofs. Long after the Germans were gone, people were forced to resettle, as the location was divided up into tribal sections for Hereros, Damaras, Coloureds, Ovambos and so on.

One day the police came to the Zoo, checked our documents and took five of us — all Ovambos — without permits to the station. When I produced my old permit, one of them shouted, 'Stupid Kaffir! You should have left long ago! What the hell are you still doing here?' 'I've been working,' I replied. An officer told me to go over to Native Affairs and get a travel pass. 'And if you're found in Windhoek after two days you'll surely be arrested and beaten.' Since I still had my old SWANLA Identification Pass, I just went straight back to the station compound and prepared to leave.

2 On the run

It was September 1950 when I boarded the train for Grootfontein. I was going home at last, after four years! The two-day trip seemed endless, especially in our over-crowded coach. 'Still,' I thought, 'it's better than a cattle car.' When we reached the SWANLA station, a railway policeman directed us to the camp. It was a new one on the east side of town; much bigger, with more than fifty *pondoks*. I soon found, however, that it was only the size and location that had changed.

It was 4 in the afternoon. We were assigned *pondoks* and an hour later a call came over the loudspeakers: 'Newcomers from Windhoek! Those who just arrived! You must now go pick up your rations!' We got in a long queue, close to five hundred of us, each man holding his own bag for the ration of mealie meal. Later, I followed some old-timers to the bush for firewood. After supper I went to sleep early, at about 8, wrapped in my blankets on the cement floor of the *pondok*.

The camp had been moved further from town after European residents complained that contract workers were making too much noise. It was a sad joke. We were over 5,000 men with absolutely nothing to do but sit and wait in open compounds outside the filthy *pondoks* — except when it rained. Many had been working in South Africa, in the Transvaal mines or Johannesburg. It was natural that when they got together with friends and countrymen again, after being away for up to three years, there would be plenty of talking, singing and dancing to the *eengoma* (drums).

I didn't join in, because I'd never learned our traditional songs and dances. Under pressure from the missionaries, my parents had kept us from participating in our own traditions for fear of 'endangering' our Christian education.

But I was very interested in *onghandeka*, a sport like boxing, only using open hands. Two boys or men would fight till one fell to the ground, then someone else would challenge the winner. Some men were experts, knowing exactly where to hit. Having learned as a young boy, I was pretty good myself and won quite often. I remember one time in the compound I beat a fellow on contract to CDM (Consolidated Diamond Mines) at Oranjemund. I looked young so he thought he would beat me easily. But I went for his ankle and down he went! These *onghandeka* matches kept me occupied for hours on end. In a SWANLA camp you just had to have something like that to do . . . it was impossible to simply sit and wait days or weeks for your bus.

I was anxious to get home but unfortunately had to wait two whole weeks before getting a bus. It was an exciting moment: getting on the bus for home after such a long absence. I pictured my father and mother at the kraal and wished the bus would fly. We left at about 7 in the morning and came into Namutoni station around noon. Now we had to wait for another bus which would take us the rest of the way.

Namutoni used to be a German fortress, used in the wars against the Ondonga people back in 1908. Now SWANLA had taken it over as a transit camp for contract labourers. We first went to the kitchen for mealie meal. Afterwards, outside again, some Bushmen approached us selling meat. I bought a roasted piece and ate it with my *oshifima*. Then we waited . . . for many hours. About midnight, when just about asleep, I heard a strange noise. People around me started stirring.

'What's that?' someone shouted. 'A lion!' replied another. This area was full of lions and our unfenced camp was close to a thick forest. Some of the men went to check. They came running back shouting, 'Lions! There are lions out there!' We quickly built fires and stood guard until dawn. Finally, our bus arrived and we boarded it for Ondangua — tired but happy to be leaving the lions behind.

Around 10 that morning we drove into Ondangua, just sixty miles from the Angolan border. It had already been a long trip, but I still had a forty-mile walk to Ouhongo. Now, at least, I was back in familiar territory, among my own people.

I had with me a small iron trunk and a big, heavy suitcase. I was lucky to have such good bags. Many men had just cardboard suitcases, which always got crushed on the long trips. The problem was that mine were too heavy to carry the long distance to Ouhongo. I either had to leave them there and come back later with help from home or hire one of the many people at Ondangua waiting around for carrier jobs. I approached one fellow and he accepted the job for ten shillings.

It was a very hot day and we rested at the station until late afternoon. I bought a cooked chicken and bread, which we ate, then I said: 'Let's go, my friend. It's cool enough to leave now.' I was impatient to get home and see my family. I'd written that I was coming, so I knew they would be anxiously waiting for me.

It was a hard walk to Ouhongo. I carried the trunk, weighing over sixty-five pounds, and my friend took the suitcase, which weighed almost twice as much. I was quite strong then and could carry such heavy loads. (I don't think I could do it now.) Well, we marched on for hours till we got tired and stopped for a rest. After a while I rose wanting to go on but my friend said, 'No, let's find a place here to sleep. We'll continue in the morning.' I agreed and we found a spot to spread out our blankets in the sand and sat finishing the last of the bread and chicken. We'd brought no water and it was impossible to get some at midnight; but we were so tired it didn't matter. We fell asleep in minutes.

We went on early the next morning. Soon I began to recognise familiar bushes and trees; kinds that grow only in the north. My carrier friend kept asking, 'How much farther is this Ouhongo?' I'd point out the trees and other landmarks saying, 'Not far now, just a few more miles.' Finally we came to a dam which I knew was five miles from home. I told my friend he could leave me here as we were very close now, but he decided to finish the journey with me.

We rested at the dam from 1 o'clock till dusk. There is a custom that when one returns home after being gone a long time, one should not arrive during the day. I think this is related to certain traditional beliefs in witchcraft. My parents didn't really believe in witchcraft, but they still did certain things in the traditional way. So we waited so that I could return at night.

We reached the kraal a little after 9. I had difficulty recognising it at first, as some huts had been torn down and new ones built in different places inside the kraal. But then I spotted the six *omyoongo* and four *omive* trees in our fields and knew I was home. I looked for our big dog but apparently he had died. A new one charged toward us and started barking viciously. I thought he'd attack, but just then my brother Alexander came out and called him off.

'Who is it?' he asked suspiciously

'It's me, Vinnia.'

'Vinnia!' He jumped excitedly in the air and ran up to me. We laughed and embraced. You can imagine, after four years! Well, I introduced my friend and after talking a bit Alexander led us inside. Now the whole kraal came alive. 'Hey, it's Vinnia!' Everyone crowded around, welcoming me home and asking many questions at once.

We went to the *olupale*, the hut where people visit. Alexander fetched wood and we built a big fire. We could see one another clearly even though there was little moonlight. My sister prepared food and for many hours we sat around the fire talking, eating and drinking corn beer.

I told them about my life and work at the farm and in Windhoek, then they talked of changes at home. My brothers, Hamutenya and Issaschar, had left a few months earlier on contract to the Tsumeb copper mines. Issaschar was just sixteen. Alexander had been working as a houseboy for the railway station master in Outjo. He had some trouble with his *baas*, however, and was dismissed before the contract was up. Hilalia had started missionary school at Engela.

My father had opened up more land once he'd got a plough. He paid a lot for it at the SWANLA store near Engela. Many people had ploughs in those days. 'Even so,' my father said, 'some have left Ouhongo because they just couldn't grow enough here to feed themselves and pay taxes too. They've gone to virgin lands east of Oukwanyama.'

Next morning my father showed me around. I saw our bigger fields and the ox and two donkeys used for ploughing. But many of our animals had died during the 1946–7 drought. I used to have ten goats of my own; now only four remained. Two days after coming home I slaughtered one for a feast with my carrier friend from Ondangua. We also brewed beer for the occasion. It was by far the best meal I'd had in a long time. Next morning he started back. I went with him as far as the dam, where we parted.

For the next several months I worked with my father and Alexander. We built new huts and repaired fences, cutting new poles and fitting them into the weak spots. I also helped in the fields. There was always something to do.

In January 1951 I decided to work on contract again. This time I would try for a good job, maybe at the diamond mines in Oranjemund. I packed up, said a sad goodbye to my family and set off for Ondangua.

When I arrived I went straight for classification. Being bigger and stronger this time I got a 'B' tag. Then I waited. Finally they announced on the loudspeaker: 'Those who want work in the diamond mines, report to the SWANLA office!' There was a big crowd already lined up for these jobs. Many of us were disappointed when they announced that only experienced mine workers, with cards to prove it, could be contracted. I returned to the waiting *pondoks*, thinking that a job in Windhoek would be the next best thing. After a week, still no luck. The trouble was that I hadn't ever worked 'legally' in Windhoek. So I decided to try from Grootfontein, where they had all the papers from employers in Namibia.

With some other unrecruited 'B boys', I got the bus for Grootfontein. It was a week before they called us. 'Those of you who arrived last Tuesday from Ondangua! Bring your passes to the office!' Inside, when it was my turn, they told me: 'We're sending you to Windhoek to work as a houseboy for Mr Maree, the postmaster. Here, sign this contract!'

The following day I was on the *kataula* again, in a filthy cattle car. I tried not to bother much about the horrible conditions, but it was a very long three days to Windhoek. We arrived at 6 in the morning. I was told to wait in the room for 'Non-Whites' till my *baas* came. By 10 o'clock he hadn't arrived and I wondered if he would come at all that day. I became restless and decided to go visit some friends.

First I went to see Samuel, then to visit some other friends who worked at the Kaiserkrone Hotel. They gave me something to eat and we talked until mid-afternoon. Then two of them accompanied me to the station to collect my luggage. Still no Mr Maree. So we returned to spend the night at the hotel.

Next morning at 8 I went to the post office to report to Maree. I asked an African working at the front counter. 'The postmaster? No, he isn't here; gone on leave. But Mr van Zyl might see you.' He turned and said something to one of the Boers. The man got up from his desk and came over.

'Are you Maree's boy?'

'Yes, *baas*.'

'Give me your papers . . . Yes, you're the one. Look, your *baas* is in South Africa and won't be back for a few days. You can work for me till then. Where are your things?'

'With friends.'

'OK. Wait outside until we close for lunch. Then we'll drive by to pick up your things and I'll take you to the house.'

I waited outside the post office till one o'clock, when van Zyl and his wife came out. She worked there too. In the car she said, 'Don't worry, Vinnia. Your *baas* is a very good friend of ours. You can stay with us and help in the house.'

I stayed at the van Zyls for about two weeks. I did housework, sweeping floors, washing dishes and so forth, and also took care of their two kids when they went out. The children seemed to like me. They were excited being able to talk with an Ovambo and asked many questions about Ovamboland — what it looked like, what the children did there, and so on. We got on well and they never gave me a bit of trouble.

One day Maree showed up at the van Zyls. He'd just returned and wanted to pick up 'his boy'. I quickly got my things together and we left in his car. He had a huge house in the richest part of town. He made a point of showing me the house of his neighbour, a man named Hoogenhout, the South African administrator for all of South West Africa.

He told me he was a good *baas*, and the *missus* was too. 'And if you're a good boy, we'll surely increase your wage!' In the SWANLA contract and pass I carried my wage was written as one pound five a month.

They showed me the house and explained my duties. My quarters were out back, a brick building fifteen feet square, with one window and a door. It had a bed, two chairs and an outside toilet. They gave me an alarm clock saying I should get up early enough to make their coffee and breakfast.

I started work next morning. They seemed good people, but the work was really too much. Every day I got up at 6, worked in the house till 3, had an hour's rest in my room, then watered their large flower garden. They were very fussy about the garden, so I had to spend a lot of time tending it. At 7 I quit work outside and returned to the house, helping with the supper and dishes. I was the only servant and it seemed my day never ended.

I thought Maree would soon increase my salary, but after ten months I had serious doubts. He never mentioned a rise after that first day. Finally, I got up my courage and one evening asked for an increase of five shillings. They both got very upset, especially the wife. She accused me of not being a good 'boy'. 'Sometimes,' she told her husband, 'he just ignores me! When I tell him to do something he pretends not to hear.' She made up other stories too.

'Well,' the *oubaas* said, 'it seems you've been cheeky to the missus and haven't done your work well. So I can't possibly raise your wages.' I started to explain that there'd never been any trouble before, but he cut me off. 'I want to hear nothing more about a rise!'

Next day the *missus* said, 'Vinnia, you shouldn't have been so arrogant as to ask your *oubaas* for more money!' I just listened, my heart beating. I was very angry — especially after the lies she'd told the night before. I replied, 'Well, I'll see what I can do about it.'

'What?' she shouted. 'What do you think *you* can do?'

'I'm a human being,' I said, 'I can do what I will. You know, I'm not in a prison here!'

She bustled off and that night reported to Maree what I'd said. He called me in. 'Just what did you mean by telling my wife that you're a human being? Do you think you can *force* me to give you a rise?'

I repeated what I'd told the woman. 'As a human being, I can do what I will.' This made him furious. He swore, threatening to take me to the police for the beating I deserved if I continued 'to be rude'. 'It's just getting worse,' I thought to myself. 'Better be careful!'

'Look *baas*, I just want to work; don't want no trouble.' Eventually he calmed down, saying, 'OK. But no more talk about wages!'

I worked another three months, then went to the *oubaas* and again asked for a raise. 'When I started here you promised to increase my wages if I worked hard. One pound five is really too little for all the work I'm doing. You can't expect a human being to labour so hard for so little pay. If you think that increasing my wages will make me too rich, then you can get another "boy" for the garden and I'll just work in the house at my present wage.'

This was really too much for him. He threatened to shoot me! 'Look here, Kaffir, if you get cheeky with me once more I'll kill you! I won't take that from any Kaffirs. I bought you from SWANLA and brought you here from Grootfontein; so you'll do exactly what I tell you! And if you're a stupid Kaffir and don't follow my orders, then I'll shoot you!'

I didn't say a thing, just looked at him. Other Africans had been shot for insubordination with little fuss made about it.

From that time on I knew I had to leave. I thought, 'What the hell are you doing here, Vinnia? Forget the contract, man, you've got to get out!' Even if I was caught and punished, I was determined to leave. Anything seemed better than serving out my contract.

A few days after our confrontation, in the afternoon, I was in my room reading. It was raining so I didn't worry about the garden. Then all of a sudden the *missus* came charging in. 'Vinnia! What the hell are you doing? Why aren't you working?'

'I just finished the housework,' I replied.

'And what about the garden?'

'It's wet, *missus* . . . doesn't need watering.'

'Well, you can do something . . . some weeding.'

'OK,' I said slowly, 'I'll do some weeding.' But when she left I returned to my book. I had decided right then to leave that night.

At 8 I went into the house as usual and set the table. While they were eating I overheard the woman say I'd refused to work in the garden. Immediately the *oubaas* called me. 'It seems, Vinnia, that you just won't follow orders any more. I've been patient with you, but if you think you can get away with this you're mistaken! I'll call the police. They'll surely take you to the station and beat you up thoroughly. Then you'll realise I'm no Kaffir like your father — I'm the *baas*! Do you understand that?'

'I understand, *baas*,' I said.

'Well, then, can I expect that you'll do as the missus orders from now on?'

'Yes *baas*, you can. I'll work in the garden tomorrow. I'm sorry *baas*.'

I'd made my plans already and wanted nothing to do with the

police. I finished the dishes at 9, then went to my room. I carefully covered up the window and began packing. I left the things they provided, the alarm clock and the big sun hat for gardening. Around 11, when all was dark, I walked outside past the house and out to the street.

I made my way to the Methodist church. A friend of mine worked and lived there in a shack in the churchyard. I knocked and woke him up. 'It's me, Vinnia. Can you put me up, Joseph?'

'Sure, but what's happened?' he whispered, letting me in.

'I left the Boers . . . broke that bloody contract. Just couldn't stand it any longer.'

'I know it was bad, but what are you going to do now?'

'Don't really know. But I'll find something,' I said.

Next morning I went around to some big European companies. First Pupkewitch & Sons, a big importer of building materials. I told the man in the office that I wanted a job. 'And just where the hell have you come from?' the man asked. I said I'd finished a contract in Mariental and wanted work for a few days in Windhoek to earn some money for my trip back to Ovamboland.

'Where's your pass? You know we're not allowed to take on boys without passes.'

'I don't have it with me,' I said. 'It's at the station with the rest of my things.'

'Well, I don't know . . . we need lorry boys; suppose you can do that work. Go see the foreman out back, near the lorries. He'll show you what to do. But tomorrow bring your pass so we can take you on officially.'

'OK,' I said, 'thanks. I'll bring it tomorrow.'

I found the European foreman and said I'd been sent from the office. 'Good!' Pointing to one of the lorries, he said, 'That one's going to the station now. Go with those boys!'

We drove to the railway station and collected a load of large window panes from South Africa. Then we returned and unloaded them at the warehouse. We went back to the station, loaded up, and again returned to the warehouse. This continued all day; back and forth, loading and unloading heavy glass panes. It was very hard work and I remember it well.

That night I returned to the church and told Joseph about my job.

I'd been lucky to get one right away like that, he said. But I was anxious about having to bring in my pass the next morning. 'I can't just walk in and show them that I've broken my contract!' Joseph suggested I go straight to work on the lorries; the man might not remember about my pass.

He was right. Next day I joined the others, put on some overalls with 'Pupkewitch & Sons' written across the chest and started to work. I looked just like the rest of the workers and was never again asked about my pass.

I lived with my friend Joseph in his place behind the church. It was quite safe there because no one was ever around to see me coming or going.

I worked the five weekdays plus half a day on Saturday. I started at 8 and worked straight through till 5. We had no lunch break. When we got really hungry, we'd just stop at a bakery and buy some meat pies. In the evening Joseph and I ate together. Then sometimes we'd go visiting friends, drinking beer, and so on. Joseph got rations from his *baas*, Rev. Jenkins, but it wasn't enough for both of us. So I usually bought some bread, coffee or tea and sometimes even meat and eggs.

I was earning one pound ten a week — which seemed like a lot after my contract job. But the work was really hard, loading and unloading heavy crates every day. I wanted to look for something else but there was always the danger of my not having the proper pass.

Nevertheless, after two months, I left Pupkewitch. A friend told me I could do better at the big Kashmir Bakery where they needed people right away. 'They need workers so badly they won't even ask to see your pass!'

So I took a chance. And when I told the man at Kashmir that I wanted a job he just said, 'OK, we can use you! Just be a good boy and there'll be no problems.' He asked if I'd worked in a bakery before and I said, 'No.' 'Well, you'll catch on soon enough,' and he led me into the bakery.

Before reporting to the supervisor I had a chance to ask a few of the workers how it was at Kashmir. One fellow said, 'The work's not too tough, but these Germans are really bad.' 'Don't know how long you'll be able to put up with their bad-mouthing,' another said. 'There used to be a lot more of us but many have run away.'

There were now twelve men at Kashmir working machines which used to employ up to fifty. It was a huge bakery supplying the whole of Windhoek. Bread, cakes, everything. The supervisor spotted me and came over. 'Can you speak German?' he asked. 'No, Afrikaans,' I replied. 'OK, then get to work!' he shouted in Afrikaans. 'You've been standing around since you got here.' 'But nobody has told me what to do yet,' I said. 'Just get to work, Kaffir, and watch your mouth!' He was red in the face.

I went over to the nearest machine, a dough mixer, and started helping one of the fellows there. I worked till 9 that night, then another shift came on. When our shift returned at 9 in the morning, I found the night workers still going. Night and day the machines ran continuously, tended only by two shifts. It was really exhausting and boring work, tending to noisy machines for twelve straight hours.

After a month or so at the bakery I'd saved seven pounds. With the eight pounds I'd saved from Pupkewitch's I figured I could now leave Kashmir and try for an easier job, even if it didn't pay as much. As before, I left without notice — which wasn't really necessary since I'd been working there illegally anyway.

A few days later I found a job in a small grocery and general store run by an old German couple named Jacobson. My job was to clean up the shop, stock shelves, prepare orders, and so on. I heard they'd hired a new 'shop boy' practically every month and thought: 'Well, this is probably another bad one.'

They hadn't asked for my pass and I soon learned to stay out of their way. After about a week, however, Mrs Jacobson asked about my pass. I made some excuse for not having it with me but she said, 'Today after work you go get it and take it to the police. They'll give you a work permit for me to sign. I don't want no trouble about my shop boy being illegal.'

Actually she knew nothing about work permits; they come from Native Affairs, not the police. I couldn't tell her that, though. I just said, 'OK, I'll bring it tomorrow.'

But what was I to do? I couldn't go to Native Affairs, much less to the police. I might as well have turned myself in for breaking contract! That night I asked Joseph about it. He again suggested I just go to work and ignore the whole thing. So next morning I went

to the shop and started work as usual. Eight to 6 and not a word
about the pass. She'd forgotten already.

I felt pretty good about getting by again without a pass and
decided to go out that night and visit friends. I was walking over to
the Metropole Hotel with a friend named Festus when all of a
sudden a white policeman comes up and stops us.

'Where are you two going?'

'To the station *baas*,' I answered. 'We're leaving for Ovamboland
tonight.'

'Give me your passes!'

'Sorry *baas* . . . they're at the station with our things,' Festus said.

'Not very likely!' the man sneered. I knew that meant we were
headed for the police station.

Inside the charge office they told us we'd been arrested for being
out without our passes. Festus, however, had an Identification Pass
proving he was still on contract in Windhoek. He showed it to the
sergeant and was released. Then two constables began questioning
me. I just stuck to my story. Finally they said, 'OK, let's go to the
station and take a look at your pass.' I knew they were serious and
wouldn't fall for any tricks. Outside I said, 'Look, I have nothing at
the station; I wasn't really leaving tonight.'

They shoved me back inside and into a back room. 'We've had
enough of your Kaffir lies!' one of them shouted. The other grabbed
me by the jacket and hit me in the stomach. I doubled over and fell
to the floor. The first tried to kick me but I grabbed his leg and threw
him against the wall. Before I could get up, however, they both
jumped in and furiously started beating me. They were careful not
to damage my face; it wouldn't have looked good in court. But they
really hammered at my stomach and back. Finally, I was beaten
unconscious.

The next thing I knew cold water was pouring over my head and
I almost got sick. The pain in my stomach was horrible. I pulled
back from the water and found two African policemen holding me
by the arms. Seeing I was conscious they dragged me back into the
charge office. The Whites took over again. 'What's your name?'
'Where are you from?' 'How did you get to Windhoek?' 'Where have
you worked?'

I gave them a false name and said I was from South Africa. 'I just wanted to find work for a few weeks and then return home.' Just then a third constable came in with a big record book. He showed it to the others, then they opened it in front of me. I saw my photo with my name and contract record written underneath.

I'd heard about this book before. It contained information on all contract workers in Windhoek. I knew there was no chance for me now. They checked through the list of runaways and, sure enough, Maree had reported me missing.

'So, nothing but lies, you bastard!' The station constable grabbed me and threw me down on the floor. Then they started kicking me again — in the stomach, back, kidneys, all over — until I couldn't move. It lasted maybe five minutes, but it seemed like hours.

After the beating I was handcuffed and turned over to two African policemen. They took me to the goal, about half a mile from the station. As I walked, every step seemed like a mile.

They locked me in a cell with twelve others. It was about 1 o'clock in the morning. I recognised a few of the prisoners. All of us were contract workers who'd been caught in a 'clean-up operation' to arrest everyone in Windhoek without valid passes. When someone asked what had happened to me I found I was barely able to talk. I could hardly breathe and was in very great pain.

That first night was really miserable, thirteen of us packed into a cell about fifteen feet square. One tin bucket for a toilet; filthy blankets, full of lice and bugs. I took my place with the others sitting on the cement floor against the walls. Some were sleeping, but the stench, bugs and pain kept me awake most of the night.

Before morning the lights came on. (The only daylight would come though a small window twelve feet above us.) Then some guard started playing with the light switch outside. On and off, on and off went the bright lights — it was a strange torture. Then a heavy knock and the door swung open. 'Wake up you bastards! Come on out, all of you!' We filed out — for what reason I didn't know. 'Form a line, here!' He then counted us and shouted, 'Back into your cell now!'

Twenty minutes later he came back and repeated the thing with the lights; on off, on off . . . Then the door swung open, '*Kom uit! Bliksemse donders!*' (Come out, you scoundrels) We formed a line and he counted us again. 'Back inside!'

They left us alone till about 8 when each cell had to carry its pot outside to the municipal lorries. As the last prisoner to arrive, I was made to carry out our pot — that was the rule among prisoners. The thing was so full it spilled over the side as I walked. Somehow I managed it.

Then they brought in breakfast — cold porridge. It had been made several hours earlier and by the time we got it the fat they put in had hardened. I forced myself to eat some, not knowing if I'd get anything else that day.

Later the police came and we were again called outside. A constable read the names of those going to court and luckily I was one of them. Handcuffed, we were taken to the courthouse and put in a waiting cell. At 10 a.m. we were led into court. Maree was there.

'Vinnia Ndadi!' I was the first called. The prosecution was brief, stating that I'd broken my contract with Maree and run away on 13 March 1951. The magistrate asked me whether I was guilty or not. I said I wasn't guilty. 'Perhaps I broke the contract, but my *baas* was very bad. I couldn't keep to the contract if the *baas* didn't treat me decently — like a human being.'

I had to argue my own defence. Pass law and contract violations were so common, you know, they didn't bother about defence lawyers. The 'trial' was a mockery; there was never any doubt about the verdict.

The magistrate said, 'You are guilty because you ran away from your *baas* with five months left on your contract.' Then he turned to Maree and asked if he wanted me back.

'No! I don't want him back again.'

'Do you want him sent to Ovamboland?'

'I don't care, you can send him back.'

'Your *baas*,' the magistrate said, 'doesn't want you so you'll be held under arrest and taken from Windhoek to Ondangua. In addition, you'll pay a fine of one pound for being in Windhoek without a pass.' I paid the fine and was handed over to a constable.

At the Native Affairs building I found more than twenty Ovambos sitting in chains outside. I was ordered to sit down too but wasn't chained along with the others. Around noon a friend from the Metropole Hotel came by and left some food for me. He'd heard I'd been tried and taken to Native Affairs. I ate a little but the guards kept most of it for themselves. As they ate I asked if I could go wash my hands and they said 'OK.' I walked to the water tap around the side of the building and my friend Erastus followed me. He'd been arrested soon after I was picked up and arrived at Native Affairs just after me. We were the only Ovambos left unchained. I don't know why.

Once out of the guards' sight, as I washed, I whispered quickly to Erastus: 'Let's get out of here! There's no telling what they might do with us on the way to Ondangua!' Erastus looked worried. 'Look,' I said, 'they can't see us now. Let's go to the back and make a run for it!'

Quickly we ran around the other corner, jumped over the fence surrounding the Native Affairs building and took off down Kaiserstrasse. Soon we heard yells. 'Stop!' They started chasing us and I expected a bullet in the back at any moment. We made it, however, to the Terrace Motors Garage and ducked inside. Behind the garage we spotted a big sewer pipe. Erastus said it led underground to the railway station. We jumped in quickly and started crawling on our hands and knees. Soon we heard police talking near the mouth of the pipe. Apparently we'd lost them, as no one followed us into the sewer pipe.

We crawled along. It was so dark we couldn't see each other. The pipe was dry but very hot and with little air, especially near the middle. Soon we were exhausted. Then, seeing a little speck of light at the other end, our morale rose and we kept going.

Finally we were out — tired, sore, dirty, but very happy there were no police around.

We quickly went into a nearby clinic and phoned Elizabeth House, where my friend Kaula worked as a gardener. They said he was at home. We ran to his place and found him in his room eating lunch. He asked us in and still out of breath we explained how we'd just escaped from the police. Seeing the shape we were in, Kaula went out and got some meat pies and *karie* beer. Meanwhile, Erastus and I cleaned ourselves up. I was still in pain, but after a little food and beer I began to feel better.

We rested in Kaula's room till 8 p.m. Then, cautiously, we went our separate ways in the dark. I went to the Metropole Hotel, where my friends were surprised to see me — they'd figured I was on my way to Ondangua by now. I told them how Erastus and I escaped from Native Affairs, where men were chained together like animals.

It had been close — and dangerous — but at least I'd avoided that police escort to Ondangua. For breaking my contract I'd surely have been charged again at Ondangua, under another set of laws, then taken to our headman at Ouhongo. He would then have had to punish me, and it was this I feared most. I spent that night with my friends at the Metropole. In the morning I told them I was going to SWANLA to ask for a travelling pass to Ovamboland. 'What?' they exclaimed. 'You can't do that! They'll probably already have a report from the police. They'd just arrest you again!' 'But I've got to leave Windhoek,' I replied, 'and the sooner the better. Besides, I know some fellows who got passes like that from the SWANLA railway compound office.' 'Well, good luck,' they said.

There was one Boer in the SWANLA office. I told him my *baas* just left for South Africa and had accidentally taken my pass with him. 'He'd been keeping it while I worked for him,' I explained.

'You're a contract boy, are you?'

'Yes, but my contract is up and I would like to go back home.' I was lucky. It worked! The man gave me a travel pass to Grootfontein. It wasn't a government document like the Identification Pass (IP) but would at least get me part of the way home.

Back at the hotel I told my friends and then said I was anxious to go. I regretted leaving them, but staying in Windhoek would be too dangerous. And I still wasn't feeling well; I kept getting pains in my ribs and kidneys. One of the men suggested I go to hospital before leaving. That, however, was impossible — I would need a letter from my *baas* just to be seen, much less get treated.

At 6 the next morning my friends took me to the railway station. The court fine had taken much of my savings so they paid for my ticket — it cost two pounds seventeen. We said our sad goodbyes and they returned to work. Two long hours passed as I waited for the train, constantly looking around for the police.

I arrived in Grootfontein two days later. As usual I was taken to the compound by SWANLA's railway police. At the office they first demanded my IP. I gave them the travel pass and said my IP had been lost. 'How?' they wanted to know. I made up another story. I was by now getting used to telling lies. That's the only way one can survive in that system. This time, however, they didn't believe my story. They were going to check back with Windhoek officials.

A week later I was called to the office. 'Look,' the Boer snapped, 'what you told us was plain rubbish! You've got no IP because you ran away from your *baas*.'

'Yes' I replied, 'I did run away . . . there was a misunderstanding. But I went back and then my *baas* said he didn't want me any more.'

'No more lies, Kaffir! You were arrested off the street!'

'Yes, but I was taken to the magistrate and my contract was legally terminated.'

'And then you ran away again!' He paused, looking at me with contempt. I was expecting the worst: he'd have me arrested, and then anything could happen!

But he turned instead to an African clerk and ordered him to prepare me a new IP. I waited nervously till I got my pass. Then I quickly headed out the door. The Boer shouted after me, 'Watch your step, Kaffir! Any more trouble with you and we'll make it tough!'

Outside I relaxed a little. I finally had an IP. Still in pain, especially the ribs, I waited a week for the bus. I was glad to be leaving Grootfontein and all my contract troubles.

3   Strike!

Back at Ondangua I found something new. A few rich Africans with lorries were transporting contract workers from the station. Walking, carrying your things all the way to Ouhongo, was no longer necessary. For one pound five I got a ride to Omafo station and I walked the last eight miles home.

Everyone was happy to see me. Before my arrest I'd written about my contract troubles. I told them the whole story. Then we talked about Ouhongo. All my brothers were away, working at the Tsumeb mines, but everyone at home was getting by. They were in good health, no malaria . . . Sitting by the fire in the *olupale*, listening to my father and mother, I began to relax again and forget what I'd gone through in Windhoek.

In the days and weeks ahead I slowly recovered from my beating. Sometimes I got pains while working in the fields, but it wasn't serious.

Soon after my return I went to see some old boyhood friends who'd also just come home from contract jobs. A few had been to the South African mines, others to Walvis Bay working in the fishing industry. We spent many hours relating and comparing our experiences and talking about old times.

One of these fellows was getting married and he asked me to be his *oshinghumbi* — best man and witness. It was to be a Christian wedding, though the *oshinghumbi* is part of the traditional Ovambo marriage ceremony. On the appointed day we all walked to the church at Engela. There was a huge crowd. A wedding in Ovamboland is a very big affair. Even people who didn't know the bride and groom came and joined in when they heard the traditional wedding songs.

After the ceremony and singing in church we went to the home of the bride. That's the custom. First, the married couple were called to a special hut in the kraal. They ate and drank beer while the rest of us waited outside under the trees. After a while they announced: 'Everyone may now enter the kraal.' We found special places prepared for the two *oshinghumbi* (the bridesmaid is also called *oshinghumbi*) and close friends. The celebration went on till about 8 p.m. when the bride's father asked everyone to leave. At night people sometimes got drunk and started making trouble. He didn't want that to happen and spoil the wedding feast.

Singing again, we started off for the groom's house. It was about eight miles. The bride walked ahead very slowly, setting the pace. She became like a queen on her wedding day, with the groom her king. We even addressed them by using special blessed names and phrases.

We arrived around 11. The group was smaller now, but another feast had been prepared. The men slaughtered a big ox and there was plenty of *oshifima* and beer. We celebrated until after 1, when only the *oshinghumbi* and relatives were left.

I really enjoyed the wedding and was very happy to be an *oshinghumbi*. It was my first time and I was glad to gain the experience. Then when I got married I'd know how to handle things. One always learns from others.

Two weeks after the wedding I left again for Ondangua. It was January 1953. I'd only been home since September 1952 but it was time for me to seek another contract. Money for taxes and other things was running short. Previously I'd considered going to South Africa. My friends told me about the treatment there, however, and I changed my mind. They'd been worked like animals and some returned home very sick, suffering from tuberculosis and other diseases. I decided instead to try for a contract in Windhoek. Having had some experience there, I figured I could get by.

My parents were unhappy when I told them my plans. They were afraid for me, considering what happened the last time. But I was now a grown man and they respected my judgement. 'Yes, you must go to work,' they said, 'but be very careful.'

I left one morning with two friends. We walked to Omafo and got a lorry to Ondangua. Arriving around 1 p.m., we went straight to the waiting compound. Rain was pouring down. We'd have to sleep in the *pondoks* that night, contending with the bugs and filth.

We put our money together to buy some meat, bread, mealie meal and firewood. There were no forests nearby, so the lorry drivers loaded up with wood from around Omafo and sold it at the *pondoks*.

We waited a couple of days, hoping for some of the better-paying jobs in Windhoek, Oranjemund or Walvis Bay. As before, the mines and fishing industry were reserved for already experienced workers. I was again classified as a 'B boy' — which disqualified me anyway for mine work. Finally, after several days, we decided to go straight to Grootfontein.

We took an early morning bus and arrived in Grootfontein around 5 p.m. After a week I was called in and told to report to a shop in Luderitz. It wasn't what I'd hoped for, but a shop job was at least better than work on a farm. I said goodbye to my friends and boarded the *kataula* next morning.

Two days later I was in Windhoek. I had a couple of hours before catching my next train south, so I left my bags at the station and hurried to look up some old friends. I found a few of them at the Grosshertzog Hotel.

'Well, Vinnia, where are you off to now?'

'Luderitz. I'm going to work in a shop.'

'A shop?'

'Yes. I don't know what sort of shop. Owned by a German — that's all I know.'

'I see . . .' They glanced at one another; then one spoke up: 'You don't really want to work *there*, do you? Luderitz is a very cold place, you know. Why don't you stay in Windhoek?'

'If I stay here I may not get a job — and I don't want to go through all that with the police again.'

But they kept urging me to stay. 'Don't worry, Vinnia, you'll surely find work here eventually. And we'll put you up.' I began to consider it. I asked about the general job situation in Windhoek.

'Well, just as you left it. The police are still hunting those without passes. But if you got a job in construction, where they don't care much about passes and such . . .' They were persistent.

Finally I agreed. I was reluctant, but I didn't really want to go to Luderitz. We picked up my things at the station and I spent the night at the hotel.

Next morning I went looking for a job. My friends recommended

Thromb Brothers, a big construction company which usually needed workers. I went there first and was immediately accepted. They did ask for my work permit, but I just told them right out that I didn't have one. It didn't seem to bother them much. (I soon found out they'd hired many workers without permits.)

'We'll take you,' the man said, 'but we're running a risk, you know. If the police find you working for us, we'll be fined . . . and you'll be arrested — so watch your step.' I said I would. 'We don't make the laws,' he added, 'we just want to get our work done with no troubles.'

I started that day, as a *lang hander* — one who assists the brick-layer, bringing fresh mortar, handing up bricks, and so on. (In English *lang hander* means 'one with long hands'.) I would get one pound ten a week — less than those with permits, 'because if you're arrested, we'll have to pay the government too'.

I joined a crew building houses in Klein Windhoek, a white suburb. We worked six days a week, from 8 till 6 with a half-hour for lunch. After work I'd go to a nearby shop for food, then return to the construction site and prepare my meal. I slept right there. You see, at each new site we put up a small hut for someone to stay with the tools and materials overnight and I always volunteered. It wasn't very comfortable but it solved my housing problem. Most of the others lived in the locations. A few like myself had to rely on friends, usually staying at the hotels.

I didn't visit my friends much now. It was too dangerous. When I did go to town I stayed away from lighted roads and made my way through the bush between Klein Windhoek and the city. In town I was especially careful to avoid places where you most often ran into police. Klein Windhoek wasn't safe either. Being a white area it was patrolled all the time.

Thromb Brothers was run by Afrikaners, two brothers who had fought in World War II and, like all Whites, received plenty of compensation. From this they started their construction business. Towards African workers they behaved just like other Boers, but I tried to ignore their insults and abuse. Just so I got my one pound ten.

I started work in February. In April I got very bad news from home — my sister Hilalia had died! I was shocked. She'd been fine just three months ago. Healthy, happy . . . and she was only seventeen. My parents wrote that she took sick just two days before she died. It was called 'blood fever', something like her heart rejecting blood — but nobody knew for sure. She died at Engela Hospital. Maybe in South Africa she would have been saved, but medical practice at Engela was very poor. People died of very common illnesses there. Often they just ran out of medicines!

I worked a couple more weeks, earning just enough for transportation back home. On 19 May I took the train to Grootfontein. I had no pass but managed to avoid SWANLA police and get the bus to Ondangua. There I hired one of the lorries and left for Omafo.

When I got home I called inside and everyone came out to greet me, including my brothers who were home now. We went in to the *olupale* and my mother prepared food. We ate and talked about my experiences in Windhoek, then my father explained how Hilalia had died. Though it was good to be back with my family again, it was a sad time. Next morning I went with my father to Hilalia's grave at Engela cemetery and paid my last respects.

I immediately began working in the fields with my brothers. May to mid-June is harvest time so we were very busy. During the next three months we talked a lot about our various contract experiences. I told them about Windhoek and how I'd broken my contract to Luderitz. They talked about Tsumeb, where Hamutenya and Issaschar worked as clerks and Alexander as an interpreter at the mine hospital.

I remember they spoke about one incident quite a lot. It happened the year before, in 1953. The mine workers were illegally brewing beer in the compounds. In Tsumeb Africans weren't allowed in bars, hotels or restaurants and beer of any kind was strictly prohibited. So the only refreshment they had was this so-called 'Kaffir beer'. It was prepared on Friday and was ready for the workers' off-hours on Saturday afternoon and Sunday.

Evidently the police were tipped off. One Sunday a bunch of armed police came charging into the compound, led by a Sergeant Ellis. They fired 'warning shots' in the direction of those gathered at the back drinking beer. One man was killed and another seriously wounded. The crowd scattered, but then some of the workers started throwing stones, smashing police car windows. The shooting started again, but just as the sergeant shouted an order for his men to stop, he got a stone square in the face and fell to the ground. The police, however, were now surrounded closely by hundreds of angry workers demanding that they come with them to the compound manager. They had little choice.

The manager was furious. He hadn't called for the raid or even known about it. He told the workers it was all a mistake. Then he returned with the police to where the sergeant still lay. They lifted him into the manager's car and drove off to the hospital, not caring about the wounded worker, who had to be carried by his comrades to the hospital three miles away. The man was bleeding badly and later died.

'Why', I thought angrily, 'hadn't the workers attacked the police?' But the answer was obvious.

My brothers had many stories to tell about Tsumeb. In general, their work and lives had been a little easier than mine. They'd stuck to the rules of their contracts and never had any special trouble with the police. Their pay was better too. It was their third term of contract with Tsumeb and they got two pounds a month. Slave wages, really, but a lot compared to most contracts.

In August I decided to leave again. We needed many things at home, including tools and cattle. Also, I was thinking of getting married some day. Though I had no steady girlfriend yet, or any savings, I looked forward to having a modern wedding like some of my friends. But that would remain a dream until I earned enough money on contract.

I said goodbye to my family, set out for Omafo and again caught the lorry to Ondangua. At the SWANLA recruiting office I asked to go straight to Grootfontein. They agreed and directed me to the SWANLA doctor, a white South African this time. I was again classified 'B'.

Next morning I took the bus. The Grootfontein office had notices from all employers who wanted people from SWANLA, but again I found no openings in the good industrial jobs like mining and fishing. Instead, I was assigned to a hotel in Rehoboth. Unlike before, my ticket had already been sent; so next morning I found myself on the train to Rehoboth.

On the way I had an attack of diarrhoea — probably from some bad food I'd eaten since leaving home. I was lucky to be in a coach with a toilet. Sometimes I was there for an hour or more and people kept knocking and complaining. If I'd been in the cattle car, I would really have suffered — not even a bucket, you just had to wait for the next station. Don't know what I'd have done — probably jumped off.

By the time I reached Windhoek to change trains I was so sick I could hardly stand. I'd had a running stomach for over twenty-four hours. I made my way to a chemist's shop and bought some tablets. I took four and returned to the station, where I waited all afternoon.

At 6 p.m. I boarded the train for Rehoboth and travelled the whole night, arriving around five in the morning. The tablets had worked and the pain had gone. Now I was hungry, I hadn't had a bite to eat since Grootfontein. I went into the shop at the railway station and bought some biscuits and tea.

All day I sat in the waiting room. Apparently my *baas* had forgotten to pick me up, and I was still too weak to walk the fifteen miles into town. Finally I phoned the hotel. Half an hour later my *baas*, a Mr Pekalski, drove up. He demanded to see my papers, making sure I was really his 'boy' from SWANLA.

On the way to town he asked if I knew anything about hotel work. I replied in Afrikaans: 'Yes. I used to be a waiter at the Zoo Cafe in Windhoek.' 'Good,' he said, 'our waitress is a bad one and cheeky. I'll fire her; you can take over the job.'

The South West Hotel was right down in the town. Pekalski took me out back to a *pondok* for contract workers. 'Report tomorrow morning. My wife will show you what to do,' he said.

I shared the *pondok* with three other Ovambos. We got talking and they told me about the set-up there. They worked the rooms and kitchen. The waitress was a Coloured woman from Rehoboth. Of course, she wasn't on contract, as that was strictly for men. I wondered about this woman I was replacing, but they didn't have much to say about her. Coloureds and Africans weren't allowed to mix. That's why the South African government made Rehoboth a 'reserve area' for *Basters* — their term for Coloured people.

I worked at the hotel for eighteen months — seven days a week. I started in the dining room at 8 and worked straight through the lunch rush. At 3, after an hour's break, I prepared the tables for dinner. I generally finished around 10, though sometimes there'd be a party and I'd have to work till well after midnight.

For this I was getting only one pound fifteen a month. After nine months I asked for a rise. I'd been working hard, hoping to show I deserved an increase. I spoke Afrikaans very well now and there was nothing I couldn't handle in the dining room. I thought Pekalski would at least consider paying another five shillings but he flatly refused. 'Your wages are set by SWANLA,' he said, 'you have no right to ask for an increase.'

'Yes,' I replied, 'but usually you judge a man by his work. If you see that I'm working nicely, with no shortcomings, why can't you increase my wage?' He wouldn't hear of it — I was just a class 'B' contract 'boy' bought from SWANLA. As I left that night I said to myself, 'OK, if that's the way it is, just take it easy — why put yourself out for one pound fifteen. No difference to me if things go well or not.'

So I started taking it easy, even being rude sometimes. Pekalski soon noticed and called me into his office. 'What's wrong, Vinnia? You're not working as before.'

'You don't know what's wrong?' I said. 'Don't you remember the other day when I asked for a pay increase? You refused. That's what's wrong, *baas*.'

'Bring me your papers,' he demanded. I got them from the *pondok* and he started reading them out loud, very slowly, '. . . so that you can understand'. When he finished he said, 'That's the law. One pound fifteen and no more! I've had enough of your nonsense now. Go back and do your job properly!'

That night I sat in my room thinking things out. I was really fed up, but what could I do? I could run away, but I'd already suffered from breaking one contract. It was very risky. I felt like fighting the man physically, but that would have been worse than running away. There were no simple answers.

A few days later Pekalski came into the dining room. Since he was my *baas*, I should have run to bring his meal. Suddenly, however, I was overpowered with anger and just glared at him. '*Was ist los?*' ('What's going on?') he demanded. I said nothing. 'Where is my food?' I just turned from him and walked into the kitchen.

Later, when the room was empty, he said to me: 'Look boy, it seems you're trying to be bigger than your shoes. Have you forgotten that I'm the *baas*? I bought your ticket myself — you didn't get here on your own. I paid SWANLA out of my pocket and you'd better remember it! Because if you continue to be "smart", I'll call the police . . . I could get them out here right now to give you a beating!'

'OK, *baas*,' I replied, 'but if you do, I'll get you first — give you a real beating before your police arrive! You see?!' I was shouting at him and he began to shout too. Pretty soon some people came to find out what was going on in the dining room. I walked out, leaving him there, then quickly took off my uniform and got into my shorts. When I came back he was at the bar drinking with some fellows, telling them about the 'saucy boy' he had. I walked into the bar, ready for anything. He looked over at me. I could see he was a little scared. 'Ah, it's you . . . Time you got to work . . . be off now!' I stood looking at him, wondering if he'd called the police. Then I realised he'd changed his mind.

That evening when everything was quiet, he came over to me and said, 'Look, Vinnia, this contract thing isn't *my* fault. I know you can and do work very hard; and it's true you're not getting much money. But that's SWANLA's fault, not mine. I'd like to raise your wage, but that would be violating the rules of SWANLA and the law.' He paused and looked at me. I didn't say anything, just stared. 'Well, anyway,' he said, 'I'll give you an extra ten shillings.' 'Thank you *baas*, that's much better.'

I still didn't like the idea of staying, but I had to earn some more money and two pounds five was an improvement.

I had no more run-ins with Pekalski and finished off my contract in April 1955. I remember it was the 24th. Pekalski drove me to the station. He said he'd like me to come back again after I'd been home a while. 'Yes,' I said, 'maybe I will.'

Three days later I arrived in Grootfontein, was taken by SWANLA police to the compound, then called to the office. They checked to see if my contract had been signed by the *baas*. I waited a week in the compound. Many were ahead of me waiting for a place on the bus. Once we reached Ondangua it didn't take me long to arrange for a lorry to Omafo. There I ran into three girls from

Ouhongo. They'd come to the SWANLA shop to buy household goods. (It was the only place near our village where you could buy sugar, coffee, cloth, etc.) They helped carry some of my things and talked all the way back to Ouhongo about happenings at home — the harvest, who'd married whom, and so on.

My family was again happy to see me back after eighteen months. My brothers were off at Tsumeb again, but my parents' grandchildren (actually, my aunt's daughter's children) were staying at the kraal with my aunt. They were young boys and looked after the cattle just as I had done many years earlier.

Harvesting had just begun. So for the next two months I was kept very busy in the fields. When the crops were in, I helped around the kraal.

In September I decided to leave for another contract. I'd been hoping to see my brothers before I left, but apparently they'd extended their contracts. I went to the SWANLA office in Ondangua for classification. Again a 'B' tag. It seemed I would never get anything better than 'B' jobs. I was still quite thin, though, and only the really 'strong boys' got 'A' classifications.

After two days I got my travelling papers and caught the bus to Grootfontein. There they told me I was going to work in Grootfontein for SWANLA. The man asked about my education. 'Just Standard 6,' I said. 'Haven't had much schooling.' 'Well,' he laughed, 'many of the boys here have had even less. If you pass the exam we'll take you on as a clerk.' I asked about the wage but he said, 'You'll see about that in the contract.'

An African led me into a different office where I took the exam. There were questions on arithmetic, biology and the history and geography of 'South West Africa'. It took about an hour and wasn't too difficult.

Later that day the man told me I'd passed and sent me to the chief clerk, another Ovambo contract worker. He showed me my job, then directed me to the *pondoks* for SWANLA workers. These small, one-room houses formed a special part of the camp, separate from the compound. They were made like the other *pondoks*, only much smaller and with no furniture at all. (Later, I bought a cheap bed.) There were twenty-four of us in these quarters and we shared a single toilet.

I was to work here for SWANLA for nearly two years. The normal contract is eighteen months, but I had mine extended an additional four months. I was earning two pounds a month. A big part of my job was registering new recruits. When they came in from Ondangua they were put into groups for the fishing industry, diamond mines, smaller mines (like Abnab and Brandberg), farms, hotels and domestic work, and so on. The loudspeaker called them to the office where they got their papers. My desk took recruits mainly for 'houseboy' and hotel jobs.

Once I got all the papers I listed their names, then took the list and papers to the office next door. There, SWANLA officials assigned jobs, matching names with the notices from companies and individuals wanting workers. When that was done the workers were called into the office and lined up. Each man's name was called and he was given a contract to sign. If he couldn't write, he made a mark with his fingerprint. Of course, there was no choosing or refusing. My office was always busy . . . thousands of contract labourers coming through all the time. I worked six days a week from 8 to 5, but often had to work on Sundays too. Sometimes job orders piled up and employers got impatient. It was boring work, but at least I was earning some money and got weekly rations from SWANLA — mealie meal and enough meat for one, maybe two meals.

I finished my contract in April 1957. This time there was nobody at Omafo to help carry my things to Ouhongo. I had just a suitcase and handbag, however. I arrived home in the evening. The family came out to embrace me and welcome me back. My parents and my aunt's young boys were the only ones there. My younger brothers were on contract in Tsumeb, and Hamutenya was now married and living in the Onaame area twenty miles from Ouhongo. He got married while I was in Grootfontein, in 1956, bought land from the headman of Onaame, cleared the bush for his fields and cut down trees to build a kraal. Being the eldest brother, Hamutenya was the first to marry. That is our custom — applying to girls as well.

At Ouhongo harvesting had begun. Those with a lot of land would be bringing in their crops until August; our work, however, lasted only a couple of months. After the harvest we built several new huts for the kraal and repaired fences and tools.

When I left in 1955 I had hoped to earn enough for my marriage.

It was not possible, though, on my low wages. Two more years of work for SWANLA and I still didn't have enough money. So 1958 came and I was again ready to go on contract.

In January I told my parents I was leaving. They agreed. I packed my suitcase, said goodbye and set off for Omafo. The lorry brought me into Ondangua at 5 p.m. I went straight to the waiting compound. It was raining heavily, and very crowded. As usual, the *pondoks* were dirty and full of insects. It was the wet season so I'd have to spend several nights inside. It was demoralising.

Then, a few days later, there was a big announcement: the Ocean Fishing Company wanted five hundred workers! Immediately everybody surged to the office. I joined in. (I'd need an 'A' classification, but I was determined to get a job in Walvis Bay.) I was a bit nervous as I approached the doctor, but this time he gave me an 'A' tag! I didn't know why, but I was very happy. My first 'A' job . . . it was great!

About one hundred and fifty of us were selected. They said that SWANLA buses would come for us the next day, but it actually wasn't until two days later that three very crowded buses took us to Grootfontein. There we were sent to the office in groups of twenty for contract signing. Then we waited three more days. On a Saturday at 1 p.m. we boarded the train for Walvis Bay. There were five hundred of us now. Some forty-eight hours later we pulled into the station and were met by the compound manager of Ocean Fishing Co. We followed him to the company compound right next to the factory. It was built like a prison, surrounded by a high wall with just one entrance. The foreman gave a short talk: 'You are now in the compound of the Ocean Fishing Co., the company you have come to work for. Tomorrow you will be instructed about your various jobs. Here is where you'll live.' He then took us around the compound, assigning groups to different *pondoks*.

Inside each of the more than fifty *pondoks* was a cement floor, wooden, double-decker beds with thin cotton-wool mattresses — the kind you find in prisons. Many were already occupied by the hundred or so workers whose contracts had been extended.

t was late, close to 8 p.m., when we were called to the kitchen. In line, we passed slowly through, getting *oshifima* on a metal plate. We ate either in the *pondoks* or outside in the yard. That day we got a little meat with our porridge, but usually it was straight porridge.

Next morning we were called to the factory and given uniforms with numbers on them. Mine was No. 345. We also got big rubber boots, as we'd be working in a lot of water. I was assigned to the cannery. And when they found I could speak good Afrikaans they made me an interpreter as well. Whenever a misunderstanding arose between the workers and the manager or cannery foreman, I'd have to translate between Afrikaans and Oshikwanyama.

I worked in the cannery from January to June, operating the machines which sealed fish into tins. They were mostly automatic, but I had to tend them continuously. The fish just kept coming all the time.

Outside, big pipes connect the fishing boats with the factory. They fill up the holds with water, then pump out the fish into the cannery. Inside, the fish are carried along on conveyor belts past the workers and through the machines.

We started in the morning as soon as the first boats came in. Some boats went out at 5 p.m., others later. The first ones usually returned around 2 a.m. The watchman then came to wake us up shouting, 'Cannery cannery cannery cannery cannery!' Which meant, 'The boats are in, get to work!' We quickly dressed and ran the fifty yards to the factory. Then we worked until the fish were finished. If, say, five boats came back full we'd work from 2 in the morning until 5 the next evening. Sometimes even till 9 p.m. — and without a single break! You couldn't stop or 'the fish would get stale'. So the machines were going continuously, belts full and moving all the time. Many men got swollen legs and feet from standing so long. Eighteen hours! It's just too much for a human being. Sometimes a man's feet were so swollen he could no longer pull on his boots.

The food was also very poor. No time for breakfast, and once the boats started coming it was work straight through till the job was done. Sometimes, if it looked like being a long day, they'd bring us bread and black tea. If we finished early, say 4 p.m., we'd eat in the compound — *oshifima*, and sometimes meat, with bread and this black 'bush tea' . . . I think it grows in South Africa.

I was getting one pound five a week. Good pay — but there was no such thing as a weekend. We worked seven days a week throughout the fishing season. We got overtime for anything more than thirteen hours a day, but it amounted to only sixpence an hour. If I worked from 2 until 8 at night — five hours extra — I'd get just two and six more. It was on the contract.

To make things worse, the manager didn't give a damn about working conditions in the factory or the workers' health — our swollen legs and the packers' hands bleeding and swollen from slivers in their fingers and under their nails. There were no medical services; you were taken to hospital in town only if seriously injured. And even then you had to return to work the same day if possible. If your feet got so swollen that you couldn't put on your water boots, you were simply given a bigger pair!.

I remember there was one incident soon after I started, an accident in the fish meal plant where rotten fish and parts like the head and fins were made into feed and fertilizer. Sometimes a boat's whole catch was bad and inside the plant there was a big tank for rotten fish. One day two men were working at a machine which sucked out the fish and filtered them on to a belt below. One man stood at the top of the tank on a plank across the middle, raking fish down to the mouth of the filter. Well, this fellow slipped and fell right into the machine. It just kept turning and ground up his leg until it got clogged and stopped. He was taken off to hospital but lost so much blood that he died on the way. It was an incident that made a strong impression on me.

Another, even more important, event was the fishery workers' strike in January 1959. Our foreman, a Boer named Baker, was really vicious — always shouting, insulting us, picking fights and so on. One day he started an argument with one of the workers and they started fighting. Baker was soundly beaten and thrown onto the floor by the Ovambo. He went straight to the phone and called the police, who came and arrested the worker. Now, when the police in Namibia hear that a Kaffir is *parmantig* (impudent) they don't even ask what happened. They simply beat up the Black man — he is *always* in the wrong, never the *baas*.

So this fellow was taken to the station and badly beaten. Then he was sent back to the factory, apparently 'rehabilitated' or put back in his place by the heavy hand of the police. I went over to him and said, 'Tell me, man, what happened?'

'Well,' he explained, 'I just refused to clean my machine while it was going.' (He worked a machine which sliced off fish heads and tails.) 'It's too dangerous. Lots of guys have lost fingers trying to do it. You start cleaning and, zip, your hand is gone. Baker is always making us do it and I'd just had enough.'

'What happened at the police station?' I asked, though I could see by his swollen face that he'd been beaten. 'They just grabbed me and started beating and kicking. Two of them. Then, without a word, they brought me back to work.'

I started thinking about what we could do to get rid of Baker. It wasn't the first case like this. Ovambo workers had got nothing but trouble from him for a long time. Apparently he was the worst White in the factory. 'Something's got to be done,' I kept thinking.

Then one day I called a meeting in the compound. I'd never done anything like it before, but felt strongly that it was time we workers stood up for ourselves. It was a Sunday. We'd finished early after working the whole night. More than four hundred men gathered in the centre of the compound. Some were still at the factory cleaning and greasing the machines, but everyone in the compound came out. They were curious as to what it was all about. I opened the meeting, speaking in Oshikwanyama. All of us were Ovambos and there's really only one language in the north, each tribe just having a different dialect.

'My friends, I called you here to discuss some of our problems. I don't think you're satisfied with conditions at the factory — I know I'm not! These Boers don't give a damn what happens to us. If we faint on the job, we're just revived and put back to work immediately. For swollen feet we get bigger boots. And this Baker goes around abusing and beating people — but if we fight back, he calls the police in to give us a beating.

'These are the things we have to discuss, comrades. Let's see if there is anything we can *do* about it.' Everyone shouted agreement and I continued. 'Now, what can we do about Baker? Just this week he had a worker flogged by the police. And unjustly! The man couldn't even defend himself! Now what do you think we should do?'

People began to speak up, expressing their opinions and making many suggestions. Finally I said, 'Well, seems we all agree that Baker has to go. And if he doesn't go, we will! We'll refuse to work if Baker isn't removed. First, though, let's talk to Vorstwall [the factory manager] and ask him to transfer or get rid of Baker.' Everyone agreed.

That night the boats arrived and we were called to work. We'd decided that everyone would go to their work places, while I went to bring Vorstwall. I entered his office and said, 'The men in the cannery would like to see you.'

'What?' He was really stunned. 'Why? What for?' he asked.

'I don't know. You'd just better come and see for yourself.'

'OK, let's go.' We walked over to the cannery and he told me, 'Call them out, tell them to stop the machines.' So I went around, 'Come on, the manager's here.' They all came outside.

'Now, ask them what they want!' Vorstwall ordered. So in Oshikwanyama I said: 'The manager asks what you want.' We'd already appointed our spokesman, an old man called Namuandi. He stepped forward and said, 'We're not happy with what's happening in the factory. For example, we work all day long, standing from early morning for thirteen or more hours without a break. Our legs and feet get swollen. But all we get is bigger boots! No medical treatment. It's so bad many of us have got rheumatism. Also, when there are injuries the only treatment we get is first aid, just enough to keep us working. Never hospital care.'

Vorstwall was listening very seriously. I think this was the first time he'd ever been approached by workers complaining about factory conditions. Finally the question of Baker came up. Namuandi said, 'Another thing is that we have a foreman who is continually abusing us. Insults, threats, even fights. Just a few days ago he called the police when a worker refused to clean his machine while it was still running. At the station this man was badly beaten, without a chance to explain what happened. They listened only to Mr Baker.

'Now, all of us want to tell you that Baker must be transferred out of the cannery immediately. We can't continue working under such a man. Since you're the manager of this factory, you can remove him. That is what we want!' Here Namuandi stopped.

Vorstwall looked up in the air, then down at the ground — up and down. Then finally he said, 'So that is your problem?'

'Yes, that's our problem.'

'OK, just wait a minute, I'll get Mr Baker and ask him exactly what happened.'

'No!' we shouted. 'We know what happened! Tell us here and now if you're going to remove the man or not. There is nothing to discuss with Baker! Just give us your answer.'

'Well, I . . . I can't just remove a man like that, without giving him a chance to explain. I'll tell you my answer once I talk to Mr Baker.'

We kept insisting, however, but it only made him mad. 'Suppose I don't remove him? What will you do about it?' Namuandi replied, 'If you don't remove him, we won't work. If you think he can't be replaced, then let him do all the work. We just won't work under him any more.'

He asked if these were Namuandi's ideas, and whether all the other workers really knew what they were talking about and getting into. When I translated this, many shouted, 'No, one man doesn't make our decisions — he is only our spokesman!' Namuandi said, 'We cannot all talk at once, so I have been chosen as the spokesman. What I've said is what everyone thinks. We are all agreed.'

Vorstwall looked up and down again, then said: 'Well, I'm not going to remove him. Mr Baker will do his work and you must go back to yours. And that's final! Now get back to your machines!'

The men gathered around and I said, 'Let's go back to work and meet again later in the compound.' We then quietly dispersed. Luckily it was a light catch that night and we finished early, around 6 in the morning. As soon as we got into the compound we gathered together in the yard. 'Look here, comrades,' I said, 'you heard Vorstwall. Everything we told him, even threatening not to work, and still he won't get rid of Baker. What do you think we should do now?'

Most wanted an immediate strike. 'If Baker doesn't go, we strike,' they shouted. 'That's all there is to it.' 'Wait,' I said, 'let's look at it more carefully. You know very well what the Boers do when a strike occurs. They'll call in police who'll surround the compound, block the entrance then come in with machine guns and bayonets. For sure some of us will die! How can we defend ourselves? We have no weapons, not even stones or bottles! Let's not rush into a situation like that.

'We can do something, however. Let's just slow down the work and mess things up a bit. Let's take up our positions as usual, but when the fish come in we place them on the belt leaving a few gaps, and those at the cutting machines let fish pass with heads and tails, and so on. That's the kind of slow-down tactics we should try! Just staying in the compound is too dangerous.'

The men listened, talked, considered and finally agreed. Then we discussed what the workers at each station would do.

Around 10 that night the watchman came, 'Cannery cannery cannery cannery!' We walked slowly to our positions and started working. A few minutes later the inspector cried out, 'Hey! Stop! Stop!' Fish were coming through with heads and tails, tins were empty . . . 'Stop!' One after another, the machines stopped. The foreman, Baker, came to see what was going on. 'The men are working, but look at this!' he was told. 'What are you men doing?' yelled Baker. 'Why these gaps on the belt, and fish coming through uncut?' The men just looked at him, silent. He went from table to table, finding the same thing everywhere. Then he hurried off to see Ross, the cannery's chief foreman. Both of them soon came out of the office — I guess Ross wanted to see for himself. He came up to me, as the translator, and asked in Afrikaans, 'What the hell is going on here?' I said, 'I think something's wrong, Mr Ross. You know yourself the men don't normally work like this.'

'Who organised this nonsense?'

'I don't know.'

'Are you sure? You must suspect someone!'

'No, *baas*, I really don't know. But something sure is wrong.'

He went round to all the work tables. (Each machine had a table with at least four men cutting, packing fish on the belt, etc.) He was shouting as he went, 'What's wrong with you bastards! Do your work right or you'll get no pay!' Then he ordered us to start again and stood aside to see what we'd do. Everyone continued, just as before.

'Stop! Stop! All of you. Go to the compounds!' I translated this for the other workers. 'OK men, let's go!'

At the compound I called everyone together. 'Things went pretty much according to plan,' I said. 'Yes, yes,' the workers responded. One man, however, was accused of filling his belt as usual. Namuandi said, 'We made an agreement, comrades, let's keep to it.

No exceptions. None of us should be cowards. Now, let's just continue our slow-down and see what happens.'

We stayed in the compound all day and the fish rotted in the boats. You see, if they stayed there for more than two or three hours they spoiled. The whole day's catch went to the fish meal plant where the men were still working — our 'strike' being only at the cannery.

At 1 a.m the watchman woke us up, 'Cannery cannery cannery!' We went to the factory and began working as before.

This time it was Baker. 'Stop, stop!' he shouted. 'What the hell is this, Ndadi?'

'I don't know, *baas*.'

'You know! Now just tell me!'

'No *baas*, really, I don't. But maybe you can call the men together and ask *them* what's wrong.'

Instead he went and got Ross. 'OK, all of you,' Ross said, snapping his fingers, 'back to the compound!' We filed slowly out.

A few minutes later Ross, Baker and Vorstwall came over. Ross came straight up to me, 'Get all the men out here! We're going to get to the bottom of this mess right now!' I called out: 'Come on men, the manager wants to see us!'

We gathered in the middle of the compound, where we always held our meetings. It was a good place, surrounded on all sides by *pondoks*.

Vorstwall stood in front of us. 'Ndadi, I want to know what is going on at the cannery.' I translated for the men. Namuandi spoke. 'We told you the other day *baas*: we won't work under Baker. You said you wouldn't remove Baker and we said that if you didn't we would stop work. And that's what we are doing . . . working as bad as your foreman, Baker.'

I interpreted this to Vorstwall, who was looking up and down again. Namuandi continued, raising his voice now and pointing to Baker, 'We've had enough of Baker!' The men interrupted, shouting, 'That's right! Get him out of here!'

Vorstwall seemed afraid we would throw him out physically. 'Hold on,' he shouted, 'wait just a minute! Exactly what has Mr Baker done that makes you dislike him so much?'

'We told you before! But you didn't seem to care. We've nothing more to say, just get Baker out of here!'

Baker was really shaken and frightened. He'd never faced a gathering of angry workers before and could see his position was very serious. It looked like Vorstwall had no alternative but to remove him. Otherwise the cannery would come to a standstill.

'I have listened to you,' said Vorstwall. 'Now, if you will return to work tomorrow, I'll agree to transfer Mr Baker.' We talked among ourselves for a few minutes, then Namuandi said, 'Yes Mr Vorstwall, we agree to return to work if you remove Baker.' For a moment Baker just stood there as the others turned to leave, head down, looking almost like he would cry. Then he glared at us with hatred in his eyes and left the compound. Next day he was sent to work in the labelling department.

When the three of them had left, I spoke to the other workers. 'This is a great victory for us! I think we have all learned how strong we can be when we work together!' Everyone was excited and happy with our victory . . . however minor it was. And I can see now that we still had a very, very long way to go. We'd got rid of Baker and handled it so they didn't call the police. But we continued to work long hours for low wages and under the same miserable conditions. It would take a much longer and more costly struggle before we could really be free from this kind of exploitation. But my awareness of that only came later.

PART TWO

Freedom fighter

4 'Will you join us?'

In January 1959 I met Peter Nanyemba. Shortly before our strike, Peter had come to Ocean Fishing Co. among a group of thirty recruits. We worked together in the cannery and Peter also took part in the strike. We talked a lot about African working conditions and politics in general, soon becoming great friends with many interests in common. Important things were happening in Namibia and contract workers were among the first to become aware of them. Peter and I, often with some of the other workers, would meet quite often to discuss political developments.

Mainly we talked about Andimba Hermann Toivo ja Toivo and the Ovamboland People's Congress (OPC). Toivo ja Toivo, an Ovambo working in Cape Town, South Africa, was the founder of the OPC. He was arrested and deported for sending a tape-recorded message to the United Nations. He'd cut out the centre of a book, put the tape inside and sent it as a parcel to New York. It was later played at the UN. This, of course, was big news, broadcast over Radio South Africa and reported in all the newspapers. I was very excited to learn about it.

I knew Toivo ja Toivo in Ovamboland many years before. He studied at Odibo, not far from Engela, and we occasionally met and talked. I remembered that he went on contract to South Africa, but then lost all track of him until seeing his photo in the papers and learning he'd been arrested. Nanyemba and I often talked about the case and Toivo's statement on the tape. It was an important moment for the Namibian people . . . and a turning point in my own life.

The case of Namibia went before the UN General Assembly and some of our people were there as petitioners. We heard about a man named Kozonguizi, who'd been studying at Fort Hare University in South Africa. He was smuggled out by three American students, through Botswana into Tanganyika and then to the UN. We followed these things as closely as possible through newspapers which I bought at a bookshop in town. These were mainly the *Suid-West Afrikaner*, a United Party* paper, and the government *Suid Wester* — both in Afrikaans. I sometimes picked up the *Windhoek Advertiser*, but my English wasn't very good. When I came across words I couldn't understand, I'd look them up in an English-Afrikaans dictionary. I read the papers closely, learning more and more about what was happening in Namibia and the rest of Africa. I also read magazines from South Africa, like *Drum* and *Our Africa*, which I liked very much. They had pictures, stories, news, etc.

Early in June 1959 I heard that an old friend of mine from Windhoek was in town. I went to see him and asked what was happening in Windhoek these days. 'Well Vinnia,' he said, 'we have a political party for Africans now, set up by Ovambo workers who'd been to Cape Town. Many of us are joining the party and everybody's talking about it. It's called the OPO, Ovamboland People's Organisation.'

'Who are the leaders?' I asked. He replied that Sam Nujoma was the president, Louis Nelengani vice-president, and Jacob Kuhangua chairman for Windhoek. And there were some others on an Executive Committee.

'What is this OPO doing?' I asked, still a bit confused. 'Is it connected with ja Toivo's OPC?'

'Well, they hold public meetings, recruit members and try to organise the people into OPO local branches. They even have membership cards. Probably somebody will be coming to Walvis Bay soon; they've already been to Tsumeb and Otjiwarongo. They're saying, "We don't want contract labour any more. The OPO will fight the South African government and its rotten contract system!"'

I was really excited. After some more talk I ran back to the compound and told Nanyemba. It was hard to believe there was really an African organisation fighting against contract labour. But soon we began to hear more and more about OPO. Its activities were reported in the newspapers almost every day. 'Leaders of OPO

* Parliamentary opposition party

criticize government, condemn the contract labour system, etc.' We followed these events closely.

Then, on 25 June, Sam Nujoma came to Walvis Bay. After meeting with some friends in the location he came round to the compounds, going first to the railway compound where he addressed a big crowd of contract workers. Then he went to the Tuna Co. compound and we were next. (The compounds were much the same and all in the industrial part of town.)

At the gate of the Ocean Fishing Co. Sam talked to the watchman, asking if he knew about OPO. The man said, 'I've heard of it, but I don't know any members.' 'Well, I'm a member,' Sam Nujoma said, 'in fact I'm the OPO President. Would you call a meeting of the workers here in the compound, so I can tell you all about our new organisation?'

Almost everybody came out. The word got around fast and the men were eager to hear. We gathered at our usual meeting place. Sam introduced himself, then asked if we'd heard about OPO. I said 'Yes, we heard about your organisation being formed in Windhoek.'

'Actually,' he said, 'we started in Cape Town, but now we are trying to bring all the people of South West Africa together in OPO.' He then talked about the need for freedom and an end to the contract system. 'We all know, especially you contract workers, that we've suffered much under this system. Our people have been forced to work for slave wages under miserable conditions — dictated by these racist Boers. Families are broken up and we're made to live in lousy compounds like this . . . . Not treated like human beings, but like cattle! One day we'll bring an end to this system, however, and will work as free men, each and every one choosing his work according to his desire and needs, without force.'

Then he asked us, 'Will you join the struggle to abolish contract labour?' Everyone shouted, 'Yes! Yes! That's what we want!' Nujoma continued. 'We in OPO want to abolish this whole system and we want Walvis Bay to join us, to set up a branch of OPO. With so many contract workers here, especially in the fishing industry, you should have a strong branch working for you. We must work together — you, me, all of us — to end our oppression!'

When he finished some of the comrades spoke up, generally expressing strong approval though a few had fears and doubts. 'We are encouraged to learn where OPO stands,' said one worker. 'I think most us would join OPO right now.' 'Then elect a branch secretary,' Nujoma said, 'and we can get to work right away. We'll send membership cards from Windhoek and everybody can join up.'

One of the workers replied: 'We have someone who could be our secretary — Vinnia Ndadi! He's our interpreter and can speak for all of us. He also led us in the cannery strike.' 'That's right!' others said. 'Let's have Ndadi as our secretary!'

'Are you all agreed on this?' Nujoma asked. The workers shouted 'Yes' — so, I was elected. It was a strange feeling — I was happy, excited and felt like crying all at the same time. The meeting ended and Sam Nujoma shook my hand. 'I'm leaving for Windhoek right away, Vinnia,' he said, 'but we'll keep in close touch. Best of luck!' I thanked him very much.

That same day I started organising our branch. First I went to the compounds Nujoma hadn't spoken at, explained about OPO, telling the men what Sam had told us. Soon, however, I found that the work was too much for one man. There were too many compounds and thousands of workers ready to join OPO. I decided to call a mass meeting at Ocean Fishing, inviting the other compounds. It was a big meeting — a huge crowd of workers were packed into our main compound. I told them I had been elected secretary of OPO's Walvis Bay branch, but that we also needed an assistant secretary and representatives from all the compounds. This was discussed in small groups, then the workers elected Peter Nanyemba as assistant secretary. The compounds would hold separate meetings to choose their representatives.

'Comrades,' I said, 'one thing we can do now is to raise some money to strengthen the organisation. We should take up collections in every compound. If everyone gives a shilling or two — even six pence — each month, the OPO will become more powerful. OPO is working for our interests and it's up to us to help make it strong!' This was agreed upon and after the meeting Nanyemba and I arranged for every compound to have its own book for recording the money collected. At the end of each month we would go around to meet the representatives and collect the money, recording it in our own book and discussing any problems. By the end of September we had a membership of several thousand and had collected over £800.

We kept this in a locked metal box in the compound. I kept the box and Nanyemba the key, but we never had any problems with security. However, having raised so much money, I decided to write to Windhoek asking what we should do with it. I feared that if we sent it through the post the Boers might ask questions, perhaps even confiscate it. Windhoek replied: send someone to deliver the money directly to the Executive.

I called a meeting of all the workers in our compound plus two representatives from each of the others. (We held big meetings like this only when necessary, sometimes in one of the other compounds. Ocean Fishing Co. hadn't made any trouble yet, but we had to be careful. Generally we held small meetings with just the representatives.) I started by telling everyone how well we'd done, how much each compound had raised, and that we had to send the £800 to Windhoek. 'We must select someone to deliver it to the OPO Executive,' I said, 'someone who is reliable and will know what to do in case of search, arrest or any other difficulty. He must be a man who can face any situation. What do you think?'

One of the workers asked, 'Why not you Ndadi?' Another said, 'We can trust Vinnia and know he's reliable.' Everyone agreed that I should go to Windhoek. I asked that somebody accompany me; it was a lot of money, very important for OPO and for those who had contributed out of their small wages. So they decided that Joshua Hilukilua should go with me.

Joshua and I left Walvis Bay the next Saturday morning. We took the 7 a.m. train to Swakopmund, arriving in plenty of time for the 10 o'clock to Windhoek. We'd got special weekend travel passes, which weren't as difficult to get in Walvis Bay as in other places.

We travelled the whole day without incident, getting in around 6. Some OPO comrades met us at the station. We got into a waiting car and took off for the location. It was still the same 'old location' — where Sam Nujoma and the others lived. (The struggle over the new 'townships' was soon to emerge — but I'll come to that shortly.)

We went to the president's house. It wasn't big; just two bedrooms (one for the children), a kitchen and a small sitting room used for meetings. Sam welcomed us and made us comfortable. He said he'd called a meeting of the Executive for later that night. We started around 11 p.m., when things got quiet in the location. Sam introduced us to the six other comrades on the Executive. All but one were unknown to me.

Sam asked me to say a few words about our new branch. I said, 'We've been sent by our Walvis Bay comrades to deliver the £800 we collected. Fortunately, our journey was without trouble from the Boers and we're happy to be here with you. I'd like to give you this money now so maybe we can count it and you can give us a note saying you received it.'

I got the bag and put it on the table. It was mostly coins. You can imagine, £800 in coins! We spent two hours counting it up. When we finished everyone clapped. 'Comrades,' said Sam Nujoma, 'this is a very great contribution! We know it's not an easy thing for men on contract to contribute much money. But you've done a very good job at Walvis Bay! Tomorrow we'll hold a meeting at the railway compound. I'm sure everyone will be happy to hear from the Walvis Bay comrades and learn how well they're doing.' The others agreed, indicating it was a good way to strengthen ties between branches. One of the men was assigned to make the necessary arrangements.

After the meeting, and before going to sleep, I thought about the next day's meeting. I'd be going back to the same railway compound where I used to stay illegally, when I was in Windhoek with no pass. This time, however, not as a contract breaker but as an OPO man working to demolish the whole contract system.

We got to the compound at 1 p.m. Over 1,000 men had gathered. We were introduced and I spoke first, trying to encourage the men to work hard so we could strengthen OPO and win our objectives. 'We contract workers must stand up and fight for our freedom! It's up to us — putting our strength together in OPO — to abolish contract labour. We can and we must win!' My talk was brief, but I was very excited and the men responded enthusiastically. Spokesmen for Windhoek branch expressed their appreciation for our work in Walvis Bay and told us to continue the fight. Afterwards we returned to the location. It was Sunday and we had a few more things to discuss before leaving for Walvis Bay. We sat at Sam's and talked about the proper way of conducting meetings, what to tell the people, what to do when the police came, what to do when OPO members were arrested, and so on. We hadn't yet been approached by the police, but they told us it was only a matter of time.

That evening two comrades drove us to the station. In the waiting room we saw a boy about fifteen years old handcuffed to a bench. We spoke to him and found he was a runaway. He'd been working on a farm where his *baas* beat him constantly. It got so bad that he ran away. He'd just been arrested and was now about to be sent back, escorted by a Coloured policeman. There was nothing we could do.

The 7 o'clock train pulled in and the policeman returned for his prisoner. We followed them to the train and went into the same compartment. Jacob Kuhangua, one of the Windhoek comrades, went up and asked the policeman why he kept the boy handcuffed. 'He can't escape from you now, here on the train.' The policeman snapped, 'Keep to your own business! Don't you interfere or you'll find *yourself* in trouble!' Jacob persisted but the man wouldn't say another word. Soon the train was ready to pull out. We said goodbye and our comrades left.

Once we started I again asked the policeman why he kept the boy handcuffed for the whole trip. 'Where are you people from?' he replied. 'What's the difference?' I said. 'All I want to know is why you handcuff this fellow . . . I have reason to ask because we're both Ovambo. He may be one of my relatives. So I'm asking.'

The man reacted just like a fascist Boer! 'If you're so kind and don't want to see your people handcuffed then you'd better discipline them so they don't run away from the *baas*! If you don't and they run away, we have to arrest and handcuff them!' I argued but got nowhere with him. Finally I left off and went to sleep.

We travelled all night, reaching Usakos at 7 a.m. We had half an hour between trains. It was cold so Josh and I went for some coffee at a small restaurant near the station. Just as we opened the door a White lady behind the counter stopped us: 'There's no Kaffirs allowed in here!' 'But we'd just like some coffee,' I said — though I knew the place was 'for Whites only'. The customers stared at us. 'OK, come around back and I'll give you some coffee.' There was a small window at the back through which they sold coffee to Africans. We went around and were handed hot coffee in cups with the handles broken off. I refused, saying, 'I never drank coffee in anything like that before, Madam! You can keep your coffee.'

'What kind of Kaffirs are you?' she said, 'From South Africa I'd wager!'

'No. We're from Walvis Bay.'

'And do Walvis Bay Kaffirs drink coffee from the same cups as Whites?'

'No ma'am,' I said, 'but I've got my own house and only buy cups with handles. You should get them with handles too.'

'You go to hell!'

Joshua said, 'Let's get out of here Vinnia!' 'Right,' I answered, though still angry. 'We don't want any trouble from some stupid Boer.'

In ten minutes we boarded the train for Walvis Bay. (The policeman and the boy were gone.) At Swakopmund we had to wait for another change and decided to visit a friend of mine. He worked at a shop owned by an old German who was really startled when we walked in and asked to talk to 'his boy'. We were heavily bearded then, which seemed strange to many Europeans. The old man said he was surprised 'to see such bearded Kaffirs'. He asked where we came from and I told him, 'We're coming from Windhoek, but we work in Walvis Bay.'

'What kind of people are you? Hereros?'

'No, we're Ovambos.'

'Ovambos? But I've never seen Ovambos like you in my life! Why don't you shave?'

'We don't have money to buy blades,' I said.

'But if you can dress so nicely why can't you buy blades? They cost just twopence.'

'Well, I don't even have two pennies. And besides, I prefer my beard to wasting money on blades. Contract workers don't make a lot of money you know.' The shopkeeper laughed and said, 'I'll call your friend, just wait a minute.' He bent down behind his counter and came up with two packets of blades. He seemed very pleased as he handed them to us. My friend then came out and we went behind the store and talked for a while.

We reached Walvis Bay at 10, going straight to Joshua's location. He was an Ovambo who'd managed to get a settlement pass for Walvis Bay. Joshua's wife prepared a meal for us and after eating I took a walk to the labour compound. Soon I found Nanyemba and told him about our meetings in Windhoek. Later I reported to the compound manager and was told to begin work again the next day.

I went back to cleaning machines, oiling them, scraping off rust and paint, and so on. The work was more relaxed now, so we could spend more time out behind the cannery discussing OPO business. Even during work hours we'd often talk and just pretend to be working. The Boers sometimes got suspicious, especially when we talked seriously without laughing and joking. Even some of the workers had misgivings about us. I remember one Coloured fellow in particular . . . really stupid. He thought Coloured people were somehow privileged; better than Black workers. He never did any harm, but wouldn't have anything to do with us.

For the next few months we continued collecting money for the organisation and holding meetings in the compound. Branch executive meetings were usually held at night in the location. We discussed politics whenever we could; talked about day-to-day problems, news from Windhoek and the rest of Africa, and our dreams of freedom in Namibia.

5 Stowaway

On 10 December 1959 a serious incident took place in Windhoek. It had a profound impact on my life as well as on the struggle in Namibia.

It started when the location superintendent informed people in the old location that their homes were going to be demolished and that they'd have to move into the new Katutura 'Native Township'. The people were angry and refused to go. Many families, you see, had lived in the location for generations. They had worked hard to make nice homes, however small or poor. Now government was going to bulldoze their community. All the work and money they'd invested would be lost — and without compensation. Moreover, the people knew they were being moved because of South Africa's *apartheid* law that Africans must live far away from the 'white areas'.

Determined to hold out, people remained in their homes despite threats from the superintendent. The location women organised a demonstration. They decided to go to the administrator himself, the man who represented the South African regime in Namibia. On 9 December the women began their march. They went through the location, down Kaiserstrasse and right up to the administrator's residence. There was a huge crowd, all women. At one point, South African police blocked them with guns and tear gas, ordering them to disperse. The women refused and the police fired their tear gas. After dispersing, the women regrouped and continued along a different route, still determined to see the administrator. When they reached his home they found it surrounded by police. The administrator, they were told, was 'out of town'. He'd obviously been tipped off. The police again threatened: 'Return at once to your location or you'll face serious consequences!' The women had made their point and they slowly headed back.

That evening Sam Nujoma called a meeting in the location to

discuss further actions. It lasted until 6 a.m. They decided to boycott the buses and municipal beer hall. Africans weren't allowed to buy bottled beer or brew their own. Police often raided the location in the middle of the night to catch those who made beer. The only beer they could legally drink was that sold in the municipal beer hall . . . the profits going to the local government.

Next morning, large crowds of mostly young people gathered outside the location bus terminal and beer hall, making sure no one broke the boycott. The superintendent panicked when he realised what was happening. He called in the South African police and some military units stationed near Windhoek, claiming on the radio that there was a riot and that he himself had been threatened. Military armoured cars with mounted machine guns moved slowly up the street of the location toward the crowds of Africans. Tanks circled the area and soldiers took up positions to protect the superintendent's office. Then, without any warning, a unit of police opened fire in the location. Youths and women resisted with bottles and rocks, but the police were very well protected. One woman was killed as she tried to set fire to a police van. Thirteen in all were killed that day, and over sixty wounded. I don't know how many died later in hospital.

We followed events in Windhoek as best we could through messengers, local papers and the radio. A couple of days after the shooting I called a public meeting in the compound. We discussed what had happened and what we should do if such a situation developed in Walvis Bay. Rumours were already flying about plans for a new township there. We had to be prepared. After the meeting, Peter Nanyemba and I went to see some comrades in the location. We discussed the actions we could take against the Boers if they tried to physically remove people from their homes. There was much talk and anger, but nothing was decided upon — it was a very intense and dangerous situation. At least thirteen people had already been killed and we had to be careful.

A week later I got an important letter from Sam Nujoma. He wanted our branch to send an OPO representative to petition the United Nations. We had one member in New York already, but he'd written asking that someone with knowledge of the Windhoek killings be sent to persuade the UN delegates. Sam felt our branch could best carry out this mission, smuggling a member aboard one of the many ships leaving for New York.

I called an emergency meeting of the executive committee. We met behind closed doors. I read them the letter and we discussed it, all agreeing that it was very important to send someone to the UN. The question was who and how. After talking a long time they finally pointed to me and said, 'Let's send Ndadi! He's branch secretary, a responsible leader and capable of manoeuvring in tight situations.' I said, 'OK, but how?'

One of our members, Comrade Maxwilili told us that some US merchant marine sailors had just come to Walvis Bay. 'A couple of them are Blacks from Jamaica,' he said. 'They're friends of mine; we talk about politics and the situation for Black people in America. I'm sure they'd be willing to help.'

'Good,' I replied. 'Why don't you go find them and bring them here.' Maxwilili left and returned an hour later with two men. He introduced them and then went on to explain our situation: 'Brothers, we have a serious political problem. We must send someone to the United Nations to tell about the heavy repression of our people. But no one can get out legally, the only way is to stow away on a US ship. I'm sure you understand. Will you help us? We need a hiding place on your ship and help to drop a comrade somewhere in America . . . anywhere. We have a friend there who will help after that.'

'We understand your problem,' one of them began, 'but it's difficult; we work in different parts of the ship and I don't know where we could hide a man. It'll be tough just getting him on board past the customs inspectors, South African police and . . .' 'I could hide him under my cot,' the other sailor interrupted, 'but how long could he stay there? If he was caught I'd lose my job. We see what South Africa is doing here and we want to help you — but how can we?' He paused, then said, 'Well, let's leave it for now. We'll try to work something out and let you know when the ship is leaving. Have your man ready.'

Next morning we went to work, talking whenever we could about the preparations we'd have to make. Nanyemba could take care of my things while I was gone — a sewing machine, set of cups and kitchen utensils; things I'd need to get married. He'd take them to

Ouhongo next time he went home. Who knew how long I'd be gone? The whole trip seemed like a wild dream. I couldn't realise what a big step I was taking or what it would really involve. I just felt that somehow things would work out.

Next morning at 9 Maxwilili phoned me. He was very nervous, talking much faster than usual. 'Vinnia, look here, these fellows say now that they can't fix it. They're afraid. The ship leaves at 10 this morning. It's the *Reuben Tipton*. Some of our fellows are busy loading it now. I've told the comrades to make a space for you in the cargo hold. It's all we can do! If you want to chance it, be on the dock before 10.'

I went to see Nanyemba. 'So the situation has changed,' he said. 'We'll just have to do it ourselves. If the ship leaves in an hour, you'd better get going!' I hurried to the compound, put on my blue overalls and white shirt, then stuffed some other clothes in a small travel bag. I took my money — about five pounds — and stuck it in my front pocket. Peter walked with me to the harbour some two miles away. Maxwilili was already there. We quickly reviewed what I was to do in New York. 'When you get off the ship, cable our man in New York; he'll be waiting.' I was then handed twenty-five US dollars. 'You'll need this when you leave the ship.' Our men had just about finished the loading. The hold was filled with fish meal; they had left a space for me between some of the bags.

A couple of dockers — members of our branch — came over and said the ship was leaving at 10.15. It was nearly 10. All of a sudden I got nervous. 'But I don't have anything to eat or drink. I should have some water at least . . . and a flashlight; it may be dark in there.' One of the comrades ran to a nearby shop and bought me a canteen and flashlight.

Then one of the workers came over. 'OK Vinnia, it's time to go! Just follow me and pretend you're a dock worker.' I turned to the others: 'Well, comrades, I'm off. Let's hope I'm successful.'

Everything happened so fast I still couldn't comprehend the seriousness of my mission. I had confidence in our organisation and representative in New York, and simply took it for granted that they would help me through any tough situations. My inexperience caused me to be over-confident.

I set off behind one of our dockers. We climbed up the ship's ladder and moved toward the cargo hold. I looked down and saw the hundreds of bags of fish meal. 'OK Ndadi, get in and hide behind those bags over there. When they close this they won't see you. Hurry now! Jump in!'

I did as he said and crawled around until I found the hiding place. Then I relaxed a bit. The fish meal really stunk, but while the hold was open I could still get some fresh air. Soon, however, a large crane set the cover on . . . a monstrous lid which must have weighed several tons. I put my hand in front of my face but couldn't see it. In a few minutes breathing became more difficult. The air reeked of fish meal. Hundreds of bags of fertilizer and no fresh air. It was also getting very hot. The fish meal gave off a lot of heat. I knew I would never live through the trip in that hold. I looked at my watch with the flashlight — I'd been there for thirty minutes. I couldn't tell if we were moving yet, but was already feeling sick and faint. I tried to breathe as little as possible. Then I heard the ship's horn and felt the motion as we slowly moved out to sea. I thought of my comrades who were watching the ship from the dock, unaware of the difficulties I faced.

My thoughts quickly shifted back to the hold; how was I ever going to get out? By 11 o'clock it was so hot and stuffy I could hardly breathe. I thought, 'If I can only last five or six hours the ship will be far enough at sea that I can try to get out.' So I lay back, closed my eyes and tried to relax.

At 6 o'clock I suddenly awoke. In the heat I had dozed off several times. We were quite a way from Walvis Bay by now, I thought. Nevertheless, I waited till 7. Then I tried knocking on the lid, but no one came. I almost panicked. My situation was extremely serious. 'What if nobody hears me? If I don't get out soon I'll die!' I took my pen and wrote my name and where I was born on a packet of cigarettes — in case they found me there dead I could be identified. I hid my OPO card in my clothes along with the £5 and $25 Maxwilili gave me. I had brought no other identification. If they caught me with my contract pass I'd be charged with much more than stowing away.

After knocking on the lid again I waited. Still nothing. It was 8 o'clock. I climbed up the bags closer to the lid and tried to lift it with my back. It didn't budge. I felt weak from the heat and the smell of the fish was making me sick. I tried hard to keep from panicking, knowing it would only make my situation worse. Then I took off my shoe and desperately started hammering at the lid. Finally, after what seemed hours, I heard steps, then voices. They had heard me!

First they removed a canvas and some light came through a few small cracks along with the first fresh air I'd breathed for many hours. 'If only they'd left that tarp off,' I thought, 'I could have spent a week in this stupid hold.' Soon I heard someone call out, 'Who's in there?'

'It's me, open up!' I answered.

'What the hell are you doing down there?' I didn't answer . . . just shouted, 'Let me out!'

They must have thought I was a dock worker who'd fallen asleep in the hold while the others were finishing up. They worked very hard trying to get me out. It was impossible to lift the cover without a crane, but they opened a small fire hatch and took out some bags making a path for me to get out. It was a big job and all the time they were working they kept asking, 'Who are you? How the hell did you get in there?' I didn't reply.

At last, crawling along the path they had cleared, I made my way to the fire hatch. Several men were waiting and as I stood up they each grabbed an arm and pulled me out. A strong gust of wind nearly made me faint, but the men held me tight. They took me to the captain's office. He had already been told and I could see he was very angry. As he spoke his lips trembled. 'What the hell do you mean coming on board my ship like this? It's against the law for us to take someone away from his country. Why must you cause all this trouble?'

'I'm sorry, sir,' I replied, 'but I must go to New York to see some missionary friends.'

'Hell, we're not even going to New York! We're headed for the Netherlands!'

'But I was told you were going to New York.'

'No, no! And why stow away on *my* ship just to see some friends in New York?'

I was still standing in the corridor in front of his cabin while he questioned me. 'Well, you see, my friends just returned to America. They had been working in my country. When they returned home they wrote saying they'd like to see me again. I didn't know how I could get to America except by hiding on a ship.'

He called me into his office and shut the door. 'Now listen, boy, I want the truth out of you! What were you planning to do? Sabotage my ship?'

'I've told you, sir, I wanted to visit my friends in New York.'

He then asked if I belonged to some political organisation, or if I had killed someone or committed some other serious crime. When he saw I wasn't going to change my story he asked to see the letter from my friends. 'I left it in Walvis Bay, sir. My friends know they sent it.'

'Well, I've got no alternative but to take you back to Walvis Bay. I'll call the railway police and let them know we're coming.'

His men searched me but found only my pack of cigarettes.

'OK, take him down to the kitchen for some food,' the captain ordered. I didn't feel at all hungry, knowing I was in real trouble. I told them I didn't want anything to eat. They saw I was depressed. 'Well how about a drink, then, it's Christmas Eve you know.' Everyone was already celebrating. 'OK,' I replied. He filled me up a whole glass of brandy and I gulped it down. It made me feel a bit better. The men were sympathetic and I talked a little more, telling them I'd really be in trouble if the police discovered the American money I was carrying.

'We can fix that,' one of them said. He cut a hole in the hem of my white collar, carefully folded the money until it was the size of my small finger, slipped it in my collar and then sewed it up again. 'There, they'll never find that money now!'

I asked one of the chaps where the toilet was. Inside, I took out my OPO card, chewed it awhile then flushed it down the toilet.

Back in the dining room our two Jamaican friends came in. They were startled to see me there . . . didn't say a word, just sat down and started whispering. No doubt they were asking how I'd got aboard and what I was doing in the dining room. They seemed uncomfortable, probably feeling guilty because they'd refused to help us.

It didn't seem long before we were back at Walvis Bay. Later I read in the newspaper that the ship had only been sixty miles out to sea; it must have been travelling very slowly. If it had been going faster maybe we'd have been near Mocamedes in Angola and they wouldn't have taken me back.

In the harbour I got in a small motor boat along with the captain and four crew members. It was still dark and soon I saw the city lights. Six policemen from Railways and Harbours were waiting on the jetty, armed with machine guns and pistols. Two of them grabbed and handcuffed me as I got out of the boat; three others kept their guns trained at me. The officer in charge asked some questions and the captain told him the details of the story, saying they hadn't found any documents or identification on me — only a packet of cigarettes with my name and some place in Ovamboland written on it. He then apologised for the incident and returned to the ship.

We drove to their office where they questioned me and made a brief report to be used later in court. I just repeated my story. Afterwards we went into the 'charge office'. The White sergeant on duty, van Vuuren was his name, had anger written all over his fat face. You'd have thought I had wronged him personally.

'And just what the hell could you have done at the United Nations?'

'I was going to visit . . .' 'I know what you were trying to do!' he interrupted. Then he took my report and packet of cigarettes. 'Why were you going to New York?'

'I was going to see some missionary friends.' 'Do you have any idea what a serious offence it is to leave this country without permission?' he asked. 'You're in real trouble now, Kaffir.' He then searched my small handbag finding only two shirts, socks, toothpaste and brush, but no papers. 'Take off your clothes!' he ordered, and as I stood naked he checked them carefully but found nothing.

'You mean you were stupid enough to leave without money? How in the hell did you think you would eat?'

'Maybe it was stupid,' I replied, 'but I didn't have any money and I just decided at the last minute to go.' He shook his head back and forth several times, finally calling in an African constable to lock me up.

'These Ovambos are really stupid, *baas*,' said the constable. 'They do nothing but cause trouble for all the Black people.'

'OK, OK Gabriel, just lock him up; we'll question him again in the morning.' I was led into the main section of the prison and put into a small cell. The room was dirty and cold. There was a thin cotton mat on the floor with two filthy blankets. It was 4 a.m. I was very tired and just crawled between the blankets and slept.

I was awakened suddenly by pounding on the cell door. 'Hey you bastard! Come on out!' I heard a key turn and the door swung open. I stood and faced two white policemen. They took me to the Criminal Investigation Department (CID). There were several men in the room, none familiar to me. One man began the questioning — I think he was head of the Department: 'What's your name?' 'Vinnia Ndadi.' 'Your father's name? Mother's? Where were you born? Where did you go to school? Where have you worked? How did you get to Walvis Bay?' I answered these simple questions honestly. But when he asked if I was a member of any political organisations, I said, 'No.' 'Do you know about the OPO?' 'Yes,' I said.

'Do you know about Sam Nujoma and the other OPO leaders?' 'Yes, I know of them.'

'Have you spoken or corresponded with any of them? Have you ever seen them in Windhoek or Walvis Bay?'

'I've seen some of them, but I've never spoken privately or corresponded with them.'

'I see. Who are your friends in Walvis Bay?' I mentioned a few, but not Nanyemba. The interrogation took three hours. (Later I learned that a South African reporter was in the room and after my release I discovered the whole story had appeared in the *Cape Argus*.) When he finished, the CID man ordered an African sergeant: 'Take this UN man back to his cell.'

That same day there was a raid in the location to pick up my friends and search their houses. At Maxwilili's they found his wife home alone. She asked to see their search warrant but they just shouted, 'We don't need one!' And that's the truth — South African police do anything they please in Namibia. They broke into several locked drawers, but left without finding anything of importance. They did the same at Joshua Hilukilua's house, the comrade who went to Windhoek with me. He too was at work. They again found nothing but a bucket of *tombo* (beer). 'What's the beer for?' they asked. 'We were going to serve it at a small party we've planned for this evening.' They poured out the beer and drove Hilukilua's wife to Ocean Fishing, and made her point Joshua out. He was taken back home and forced to unlock some drawers they'd been unable to open. In one they found some OPO membership cards which I'd given him for distribution in the location.

'What kind of cards are these?' they asked.

'They're OPO cards.'

'Who gave them to you?'

'Vinnia Ndadi.' Of course, he thought I was on my way to New York and had no idea I'd been arrested.

'Where is Ndadi?'

'I don't know.'

'But you do know him? He's the one who gave you these cards?'

'Yes, that's right.'

'We'll ask you a few more questions at the station.'

I had no idea what had been going on. Suddenly there was a loud bang on my cell door. It opened and two white men and Sergeant Martin walked in. 'Come on out, you bastard!' They led me to the CID office. I walked in, unaware that Joshua was sitting in the corner of the room.

'Your name is Vinnia Helao Ndadi?'

'That's right.'

'Do you know this gentleman over here in the corner?' I looked, seeing Joshua where he sat, pale and frightened.

'Yes, I know him.'

He then turned to Joshua. 'And do you know this man?'

Yes, it's Vinnia.'

'How did you meet him?'

'We work together at Ocean Fishing Co.'

'Well then, how and when did you get these cards from him?' The OPO cards were heaped on a table in front of me.

'He just asked me to distribute them in the location and I agreed.'

'Do people pay for these cards?'

'Since I'm the OPO secretary here, perhaps I should answer your question,' I said. 'Each person joining the OPO must pay a fee of two-and-six when he gets his card.' They could see Hilukilua didn't know much about OPO so they sent him out, happy to have the branch secretary under arrest. They questioned me further about the cards and money. I told them the money was sent to OPO headquarters in Windhoek by post.

That night I was taken into the main yard where all the prisoners were eating dinner. The compound was surrounded by a twenty-foot wall. I was told not to talk with anyone. A guard brought me some *pap*, a thin, cold maize meal porridge. It so happened this guard was an old friend, a contract worker I'd worked with in Windhoek. I was really surprised to see him there. We spoke briefly in Oshikwanyama. He'd heard about my arrest and wanted to help. I told him, 'Go to Peter Nanyemba. Tell him I'm here and want to see him or Maxwilili.' He agreed and left.

After eating I was returned to the cell. The following morning I was washing a police van when they called me into the CID office. 'So, Sam Nujoma sent you to the United Nations?' 'Who told you that?' Apparently Sam Nujoma called the prison after some OPO leaders heard about my arrest on the radio. Sam knew some people at the prison, including Sergeant Martin. He phoned Martin and asked if it was true.

'Sam Nujoma called,' the CID officer said. 'He wanted to know what happened to you; told us you were going to the UN.'

'Well, if that's so, Sam Nujoma's the *only* one who knew about it! I sure didn't.'

'Oh, yeah. Well, in any event, Nujoma says he was sending you there.'

'You should have let me talk with him; I'm not even sure he called.'

When they saw they couldn't trick me into changing my story, I was returned to my cell. On the third day after my arrest, around 1 a.m, Nanyemba came asking to see me. He gave a phoney name, saying he worked with me at Ocean Fishing Co. A guard came to my cell. 'We've got an OPO man here to see you.' I followed the guard back to the office. There was Nanyemba, looking very frightened. He couldn't even speak coherently. I told him I was really in trouble, that he should get me a lawyer quick! Nanyemba said he'd do what he could and handed me some food. The police wouldn't let me have it at first. They took the bag, then brought it back later. I can still remember what it was: bread, sandwiches and sausage. Very delicious after three days of prison *pap*.

Next day Nanyemba returned. He told me they'd gone to see a Boer lawyer named Lillian but he'd refused to defend me since it was a political case. In fact, no one they contacted would take my case . . . I'd have to defend myself. Later the police came to my cell: 'Well, you lucky UN bastard, you're going to trial today. No doubt you'll get the death sentence! And you deserve it, you bloody black communist!'

At 11 a.m. I was taken to court along with some other prisoners. Thirty minutes later the magistrate entered. We all stood. Our names were read and I was the first to be tried.

'Vinnia Ndadi, arrested 24 December while trying to leave South West Africa illegally. Do you plead guilty or not guilty to this charge?'

'Not guilty.'

Then the prosecutor called his witnesses. The first were the railway policemen who picked me up. They told how I was arrested, what the ship's captain said, and what I'd told them. When all the testimony against me had been heard, the magistrate asked if I had a lawyer. 'No,' I said, 'but I'd like to defend myself. You see, I don't think I'm guilty of this crime. I was unaware of any law that forbids me to leave South West Africa without government permission. I was just going to visit missionary friends in New York. I wasn't fleeing the country, since I intended to return. I therefore committed no crime.'

After my statement the prosecutor went on to explain more about South African laws prohibiting people from leaving the country. Then the magistrate spoke: 'According to the law, Vinnia Ndadi, you are guilty. I am sentencing you to three months' hard labour.' There was no fine and my membership in the OPO was never mentioned.

Once I was back in my cell Nanyemba came to visit me. The comrades had raised £200 to cover the cost of a fine or lawyer but I didn't need it. I told him to hide everything — all documents, political papers, financial books, etc. — in the compound. It was possible, I thought, that the Boers had another political trial in mind for me; they just needed time to gather more evidence.

And I was right. Next morning the police were at the compound wanting to speak with Nanyemba. They forced him to show them around his room, but they found nothing except some old news-papers and magazines. Everything else had already been hidden.

I remained at Walvis Bay police station for another week, then was transferred to Swakopmund prison, fifty miles to the north. We arrived at the prison at about 5 p.m. and I was taken to the warden's office. He was given the details of my case: 'You'll want to give this Kaffir special treatment. He's the one who just tried to stow away on a ship to go to the United Nations and spread his lies about South Africa. He's a bloody communist!' They spoke Afrikaans, thinking I couldn't understand. I had purposely spoken only my own language and a little English. The warden, a man named Bokram, listened and nodded. Finally he said, 'Don't worry, we'll give him the care he deserves.'

'Good. I'll check in on him within a few months.' The warden then turned to me: 'So you wanted to tell the UN a pack of lies about us ill-treating you Ovambos, eh? Well, maybe the "lifers" here will be able to clear your head.' The guard led me into a room where I was turned over to several men serving life sentences. One grabbed my arms while two others hit me in the face and stomach. I fell to the ground. The men then began kicking me in the back and head. They next took out a big pair of scissors. I was afraid they would stab me — but they just cut all my hair off. Then I was stripped and forced under a cold shower. After drying I was handed a prison uniform: a pair of shorts, no pockets or belt, and a pullover shirt with red and white stripes, no shoes.

I shared a small fifteen-foot by fifteen-foot cell with seven others. Just four high concrete walls and a floor; a bucket in the corner served as a toilet. I was the only political prisoner among the 300 men at Swakopmund.

They got us up each morning at 6 a.m. We folded our blankets according to prison regulations, then ate breakfast squatting in the compound. We had two minutes to eat — cold, thin porridge with dirty raw carrots and beans on top. (Dinner was the same.) After-wards, warders came around and beat any man with food in his dish. One warder, named Venter, was especially cruel. Once I saw him beat a man very hard with a club for having a piece of tobacco. The man was so weak from bad treatment and poor food that just one blow sent him to the ground. This wasn't the only form of punishment. Prisoners were often put in the 'dark cell' for petty offences such as folding a blanket incorrectly. The 'dark cell' was far underground and there was absolutely no light. Cold rice-water was the diet. I knew they were just waiting for an opportunity to send me there, but I never gave them cause.

During the days I worked in a quarry where we broke up rocks, then carried them to machines which crushed and ground them for concrete. We worked from 8 till 5 without a break. By evening we were covered with white dust; it was in our eyes, mouth — everywhere. We'd clean off a bit at a water tap in the yard; sometimes we'd just get started when the guards would shout, 'That's enough! Get out!'

Sometimes they worked me at the Hansa Brewery in town, loading and unloading trucks. They used contract workers mainly, but if there was too much work they'd call in prisoners to avoid paying the workers overtime.

My other job was 'digging' ditches — through rock. We had to blast the rock out with dynamite before laying the drainage pipes. It was hard work, and also very dangerous. Two prisoners were killed when they accidentally set off some dynamite. Dynamite sticks, you see, were placed in holes drilled in the rock. Each stick had its own charge and the man operating the charge had to remember how many sticks were used and make sure to blow them all. On this occasion he miscounted — one stick was left. Later, two men drilling in the area hit the dynamite and were blown to pieces. It was a horrible sight. One man was cut in half and the other had his head and limbs blown off. I learned later that these men had committed the 'crime' of being in Walvis Bay without passes.

These three months were real hell. I was never interrogated; there was no need as the police had all the documents they required. On 23 April 1960 I was released. I was in the office getting my clothes back — the old shirt still had my money in the collar — when I recognized a Special Branch man named Nathaniel Kakuambi. He looked over and said, 'Hello, brother.' 'Not me,' I replied. 'I'm not your brother.' I wondered what he was doing there talking to the clerk. In a few minutes he said to me, 'Brother, I don't think we've met, but . . .'

'I know who you are, and you're no brother of mine!'

'You think just because I work for the Boers that I support them. I'm with you. The CID sent me to accompany you back to Walvis Bay.' I'd planned to thank some people in Swakopmund who'd brought me food, but now that was impossible. We went straight to Walvis Bay by train. It took an hour. Soon I was back in the charge office. Kakuambi told the officer I was to be put under surveillance just in case I tried to stow away again. Then he took me to the workers' compound and let Ocean Fishing know I had been released. At the compound, before he left, Kakuambi asked where my things were. I told him they'd been sent to Ovamboland before I boarded the ship. I had nothing left at the compound.

I spent the night talking with Nanyemba in the compound. In the morning two policemen came and told me I was being deported to Ovamboland. I had twenty-four hours to pack and leave. The police were watching Nanyemba, but he hadn't been arrested yet. That evening he organised a mass meeting at the location. A large crowd gathered after work. I told them my experiences in prison and that the police were now deporting me. The men were angry, swearing to continue the fight against the contract system in Walvis Bay. They asked me to do the same in Ovamboland. I met with Maxwilili afterwards. When I returned, Nanyemba said the police were there looking for me. They wanted me to be at the station to catch the next train for Grootfontein. I didn't want to be locked up again — not even for one night — so I decided to stay with Maxwilili and go to the station the following day. Nanyemba tried to talk me out of it, suggesting that at least I should stay at the compound rather than the location, since the police knew all my friends and would certainly be checking there. But I decided I was better off at Maxwilili's.

Next day, when Maxwilili returned from work, he was surprised to find me still there. 'I'll be leaving soon,' I said. At 6 p.m. I went to the station but just missed the last train for Grootfontein. There wouldn't be another till 5 the next morning. I returned to my comrade's home. The police had just left, they were heading to the compound. He was worried they might come back when they found he'd lied about my being there. I was worried too, but I felt it best to sit tight.

At the station next morning many policemen were milling around. The train wasn't ready yet; they were still hooking up the engine. I quickly got aboard one of the sleeping compartments without being seen. I took a top bunk, closed the curtains and read a paper. No one checked and soon we pulled out. In a couple of hours we arrived at Usakos. I got out and mixed with the other passengers. I saw police questioning people as they came off the train, then going aboard. Once I heard them asking someone if he knew a Vinnia Ndadi. I slipped back into the same compartment right after they'd left it.

From Usakos we travelled to Otjiwarongo. There were no police. I went to see Lucas Shatuka, secretary of the local OPO branch. We'd never met but had corresponded about the work of our branches. I found him at the Hamburg Hotel, where he worked. He said he'd heard about my arrest and I filled him in on the details. He in turn told me about OPO activities in Otjiwarongo. It was a small town without many contract labourers — just a few railwaymen, some domestic servants, and hotel workers. Shatuka nevertheless worked very hard. He often travelled beyond the town to contact Ovambo workers and explain OPO work. We ate as we talked; I couldn't stay long as I had to return to catch my train. After eating, Shatuka walked me to the station. We arrived just as it pulled out of the station. The next was at 9 p.m.

I was travelling without a ticket, of course. If I bought one they'd demand to see my pass, then probably start asking questions. So I dodged the conductors, heading to the toilet whenever they came round for tickets.

Wednesday at 9 a.m. I arrived at Grootfontein, reporting to SWANLA as usual. My contract pass was signed and I went through without a hitch. I had a two-day wait for my train. On Friday I left for Ovamboland. By early afternoon we reached Ondangua. I decided to visit Andimba Hermann Toivo ja Toivo, who had been deported from Cape Town in 1958 for sending the message to the UN, and ran a small shop in a nearby village. I went in. 'Hermann Toivo ja Toivo? I'm Vinnia Ndadi, secretary of the OPO Walvis Bay branch. You may remember me from Odibo some years ago.'

'Well, it's good to meet you again. I've heard about your arrest and all.'

I explained my attempt to reach the United States and the UN. Then he told his own story, how he'd been arrested in Cape Town and deported to Ovamboland. 'You know', he went on, 'that the OPO no longer exists. We have formed a broader national liberation movement, the South West African People's Organisation — SWAPO.'

'Nobody told me! Perhaps they didn't know!' I said, a bit shocked by the news.

'Yes. It happened only very recently and we're still trying to inform people. Perhaps you can let people know as you travel north. Would you like to be a SWAPO organiser?'

'Well, yes . . . of course! I'll work as a SWAPO organiser in Ovamboland!' I promised Toivo ja Toivo I'd keep in close touch with him. He wasn't allowed to leave his village and I wasn't sure how much travelling I'd be doing, but I'd find some way of contacting him.

I returned to the compound, got my things and caught a lorry to Ouhongo. Then, home again with my family! They were all extremely surprised to see me. They'd heard I was in prison. My father asked how I'd got myself mixed up in political matters. 'I'm tired,' I said. 'Later.' After I'd rested I told them the whole story. My father was angry; he didn't want me involved in politics. 'Nothing good will come of it! When I learned you were in prison, I was sick. We've all been very unhappy.'

'I am a grown man, Father, and I must do what I think is best for our people.'

I explained more to my family about OPO, what we were working for, and at the same time tried to give them confidence in my ability to handle difficulties. It helped. They all seemed more relaxed. Mother said, 'Well Vinnia, you seem to know what you're about. This contract system has certainly caused you much suffering. It hasn't been good for any of us.'

I then learned that all my brothers had joined OPO in Tsumeb, even my married brother. My father asked if I was going to continue my political activities in Ovamboland. 'Yes,' I said. 'Well, you'll find it's different here from Walvis Bay. We know of only two OPO people, an old man named Kaxumba and Hermann ja Toivo. Hermann isn't allowed to speak at public meetings, so there's really just this one old man. No, Vinnia, there's not much you can do here.'

'I can help the old man, Kaxumba, for a start; and there will be others.'

'Well, be careful! We don't want you getting arrested again.'

'Me neither,' I said. 'But even if they do, I'll continue fighting contract labour. I've been working contracts too long. If I'd been getting paid fairly I'd be rich . . . we'd all be rich. We've worked hard. Instead, we suffer — and my children, and their children, will suffer too if we don't get rid of contract labour. That's why we've got to fight. Not much difference if I suffer in prison or on contract.'

They listened intently. 'Do what you must, son; just take care.'

6 There will be others

It was already April, harvesting time. I helped with the work and rested a week before going to Endola to see the old man, Kaxumba. He was very happy to learn I would be working with him. As we talked it became clear that the old man faced a real problem. Mainly, he had no way to get from one place to another except by foot. Sometimes he walked fifty miles to hold a meeting. At fifty-nine, this was too much for him. I told him he should request a bicycle from headquarters. He sent a letter and within a month he was cycling to village meetings.

At first, most of my work was planning and travelling. I went to Ondangua to meet with ja Toivo, then to Endola to speak with Kaxumba. When at home I worked in the fields.

In Walvis Bay I knew an Ovambo member of OPO, Simon Kaukungua. I heard he was back from contract and went to see him at Ohalushu to ask if he'd work with us in SWAPO. He was happy to be able to help. Now there were three of us, Kaxumba, Kaukungua and myself, all working to organise Ovambo people.

We held three large public meetings during this time. The first was in Endola under some trees near Kaxumba's house. The day was extremely hot, yet over three hundred people came out to hear what we had to say. The crowd of men, women and children came from many areas: Omundudu, Omakango, Ehafo, Onanhadi, etc. Some walked twenty miles. Kaxumba spoke first. He was well known, having spoken frequently as an OPO member. He spoke about the change from OPO to SWAPO. To most people it didn't matter. They said, 'Whatever will help us we support, whether OPO or SWAPO.' Then he introduced me and Kaukungua. I talked about my work in Walvis Bay, my arrest, imprisonment and deportation. I said I was determined to continue work in support of the struggle. I spoke of the need for more SWAPO leaders to represent each of

Ovamboland's seven tribes: Oukwanyama, Ondonga, Uukwambi, Ongandjera, Uukwaluudhi, Uukolonkadhi, Ombalantu. 'We need SWAPO people in all these areas,' I said. 'To organise meetings, enrol new members, collect membership fees and organise actions.' I also explained that OPO was a regional organisation, formed by Ovambo workers in Cape Town, and was a workers' union against contract labour. SWAPO's main objective, on the other hand, was to help liberate all the peoples of South West Africa from Boer oppression and win national independence.

Our next meeting, at Ohalushu, was attended by more than five hundred people. It was in Kaukungua's area so he acted as chairman, but we all spoke. There were always questions of 'How?' How were we going to liberate ourselves? Was the UN going to do it, or SWAPO? One woman asked if the South African government had the right to reject UN decisions. I answered: 'The South African government listens to no one. It is strong enough to ignore whoever it likes. They don't even recognise the UN as having legal authority over South West Africa — only the old League of Nations which gave South Africa administrative power in Namibia. The UN knows exactly what is happening here; it has passed many resolutions condemning South Africa, but still nothing has changed. No, we can expect little from the United Nations. Only Namibians can free Namibia!'

An old man then wanted to know what kind of a struggle I was talking about — war?

'Yes, there is probably no way we can gain our independence except through armed struggle. We must be prepared to fight with anything — guns, bows and arrows, spears . . . anything! War is a serious conflict — South Africa must not be allowed to oppress us for ever. We must fight back and win our freedom.'

The old man's face glowed. 'That's all I wanted to know,' he said. 'You lead, we're prepared to fight. At first I thought you meant only to continue struggling with words. But I agree — it's time we took up guns, spears, *omakatana* [machetes]!' He said he had fought the Portuguese back in 1917 with King Mandume and the Oukwanyama. And he still certainly had the same fighting spirit despite his age.

I found it necessary to talk again about the Walvis Bay incident.

There were rumours that the Boers drowned me when I was removed from the ship. Rumours often spread wildly in Ovamboland; mine made a good story. But rumours also confuse people and I warned them to beware of rumour-mongers.

I also stressed the need for unity. 'Look at the Boers. They have united in order to oppress us, to exploit our labour and our land! If we were to join as one man we could surely defeat them and overcome our difficulties.' Kaukungua, continuing on the theme of unity, gave the example of a bunch of sticks. He picked one up, 'This single stick you can break easily, but ten sticks at once? No. It's the same with our struggle: if we are divided the enemy can infiltrate and break us one by one, but if we're together as one strong force determined to get rid of colonialism and oppression, then we will surely win!' The meeting closed with handclapping, freedom songs and slogans.

Our numbers grew quickly after these two meetings and we were no longer just three men. We recruited cadres from other areas who were important to SWAPO in its efforts to mobilise the masses. They encouraged people and gave them a better understanding of South African colonialism and our organisation. They also raised funds and helped settle disputes between villagers and Boer-appointed headmen. These headmen were generally corrupt, oppressing the people just as the Boers. In fact, they were Boer agents! For example, if a man died leaving his house to his son, the son had to 'buy' the house from the headman. This was a common practice. In many such cases people sought advice from the local SWAPO cadre, who usually knew a great deal about both traditional and Boer law. He also knew what kind of man the headman was — whether or not he'd report it to the Native Commissioner if the man refused to pay. If reported, the villager would be arrested. Cadre would advise families either to pay and avoid trouble, or to ignore their headman. The people's confidence in SWAPO thus grew and they increasingly sought our advice and accepted our leadership.

My third meeting was at Omuandi. Sometimes two or three months passed between meetings. They were held only when necessary and usually centred around a specific issue. We kept moving into different areas in order to reach an ever wider sector of the population. We relied on people who attended our meetings to pass on information to their relatives and neighbours.

Our SWAPO cadre at Omuandi was Mwatale. He'd done a good job mobilising support for the movement. Among other things, he had raised over £150 for SWAPO in just a few months. Over five hundred men and women were at the meeting. Most were enthusiastic, but we also encountered some antagonistic elements — a few old men under the influence of Christian missionaries. One began shouting in the middle of Mwatale's opening remarks: 'Don't listen to these demons! They are demons! Communists!' We could have forced them to leave, but it would have only given the enemy added cause to attack us. It wasn't necessary anyway, the people just ignored their outbursts and before long they shut up and left.

After the meeting all SWAPO members met at Mwatale's place for our first branch meeting. We set up small groups or committees to study various problems, draft statements, plan future meetings and make reports, and improve our organisational work in Ovamboland. Each committee was to draw up proposals for consideration at general SWAPO meetings. Kaxumba, Kaukungua and I each headed a group of six members.

Early one June morning my father and I were harvesting crops when two African constables came up. They said they wanted to tell Vinnia Ndadi that the Oshikango Native Commissioner wanted to speak with him. I asked why, but they didn't say.

'Well, I'm Vinnia Ndadi. Tell the Commissioner I'll be in to see him tomorrow.'

'No,' they said. 'We've been ordered to bring you in today.'

'But I haven't got a bicycle, do you expect me to get there walking today? One of you will have to let me ride your bicycle if I'm to make it.' So I took one of their bicycles and they doubled-up on the other. Before leaving I turned to my father. 'Don't worry! I should be back around 7. If not, I've probably been detained.'

We reached Oshikango about 11 a.m. Strydom, the Native Commissioner, was waiting outside. He took me into an office and sat down behind his desk. I stood. He began by asking when I returned to Ovamboland. 'In April,' I told him.

'What made you leave Walvis Bay?'

'I was on contract and it expired. So I had to return.'

'I know that!' he huffed. 'I also know you were trying to flee to the UN to tell a pack of lies about South Africa. You were arrested, imprisoned, then deported here . . . and in the process you escaped from a police escort! I know the truth so don't bother me with lies. Now I'll tell you something. You'll not stay in Ovamboland poisoning people with your communist filth! These are peace-loving people, they don't want your kind of trouble. Even your own parents don't want it. I'm deporting you to a place between Okavango and Oukwanyama . . . fifty miles of uninhabited land where you can talk to the lions and other game animals!'

'Very well,' I replied, 'but remember — even that area is part of *my* country. The lions and other animals are my brothers and I'm always happy living among my brothers. But you are not my brother! I don't even know where you . . .'

'You're stupid, Kaffir! Those lions will tear you apart!'

'Then it kills its brother. That is better than being killed by a stranger who has entered your house uninvited.'

He looked at me oddly for a moment, then went on. 'I don't think you understand what I'm telling you. I know of all your activities here — how you've organised meetings and spread lies among the people. You haven't seen me at your meetings, but I know every word you've spoken.' He paused and looked at me, almost friendly. 'No, I don't think you're as stupid as Kaxumba or Kaukungua. You must realise you can hide nothing from me. Now why don't you just tell me about those meetings and this SWAPO of yours.'

'What's the point, you already know everything.'

'Do you still distribute SWAPO cards?' he asked.

'Yes.'

'How much do they cost when someone joins?'

'Two-and-six.'

'And what do you do with the money, split it among yourselves?'

'No! We buy food for people in the drought areas. Government does absolutely nothing so SWAPO is raising funds and buying maize to send. You Whites don't care if Ovambos live or starve. But SWAPO represents the people's interests. This is why we raise money.'

'Who is your treasurer?'

'The old man, Tuhadeleni Kaxumba.'

'Kaxumba! That beggar! Why can't you find a more responsible person?'

'Kaxumba is responsible. He is poor but he is a good man and honest.'

Strydom's mood changed. I'd put him on the defensive. 'Look here, Ndadi,' he said with a forced smile, 'I was angry to find you in Ovamboland. You entered without reporting to me, then you held illegal meetings, calling yourself OPO or SWAPO or whatever. You should have asked me for permission. Now . . . I sent for you to see what kind of man you are. I won't send you to Okavango now, but I'm very serious when I tell you not to hold any more meetings. If you insist on continuing your nonsense I'll send a couple of trucks and dump you and your whole family in the bush. OK, you can go now; but remember what I've told you. No more meetings!'

I walked back to Ouhongo. My family was relieved to see me. They were afraid I'd been detained. I told them what had happened.

Next day I went to see Simon Kaukungua and told him the story. He suggested we hold a special meeting to discuss it. He sent someone from his shop to inform the others. (Kaukungua ran a small general store which was very popular. Most people preferred it to the three SWANLA shops at Ondjondjo, Omafo and Endola.)

The meeting took place at Ohalushu on Saturday. There were the eleven of us: Kaukungua, Kaxumba, Mwatale and myself plus seven representatives from other parts of Ovamboland. Kaukungua was chairman. I told them about my arrest and discussion with Strydom. 'I had a gun hidden in my house and could have shot the traitors; but I decided the Boers would only use it to divide us. So I didn't resist arrest. Strydom said that if we continue public meetings he would deport us to a place like Omboloka. We must now decide what to do.'

Kaukungua spoke next. 'I'm prepared to go on with our work. We can't just abandon the struggle because our enemy threatens us. This only proves they are worried; that we are becoming effective and a threat.' Everyone agreed. We decided to continue holding meetings and planned the next steps.

In the months following, several meetings were held with more and more people turning out. For some reason Strydom didn't carry out his threat and there was no police harassment. Perhaps it was because this was a time when the case of Namibia was being debated within the UN General Assembly. In 1961 we heard that Dag Hammarskjold, UN Secretary-General, had appointed a committee to go to South West Africa and investigate the situation on the spot. The committee was to be led by a Uruguayan, Mr Fabregat. I got this information from Windhoek in a message passed through Andimba Toivo ja Toivo. I immediately went to Ohalushu and told Kaukungua.

'Let's call a branch meeting at Omuandi,' Kaukungua said. I agreed, as Omuandi is in the heart of Ovamboland. Next morning I went to Endola to see Kaxumba. He agreed with our proposal and said the branch should meet as soon as possible to prepare a statement for the UN Committee.

The meeting took place a week later. Since Omuandi is Mwatale's home area, he organised everything. Many people in his household helped — making food and seeing that SWAPO leaders were introduced and hospitably received by the Uukwambi people. Even ja Toivo arrived, violating his restriction order because he felt it was a very important meeting.

Mwatale was chairman. I told the people about the news from Windhoek; that the UN Committee on South West Africa was on its way, and that our branch should send someone to Tsumeb to meet with them. We weren't sure of their plans, however — whether they would come to Windhoek first, then Grootfontein and Tsumeb, or what. But since Tsumeb was the closest to Ovamboland we decided it was best if somebody went there. SWAPO had a branch in Tsumeb, but the leadership wanted somebody from Ovamboland to go who knew our conditions well and had a correct political position and background. There was nobody in Tsumeb who felt confident about meeting with the Committee.

When it came to picking our delegate, I was selected. I told the comrades it was OK with me, but that the question was how. The necessary travel pass had to be obtained from the Native Commissioner at Oshikango. Tsumeb is in the so-called 'Police Zone' and a special pass was therefore required.

'Friends,' I said, 'you know I'm under restriction here; not allowed to leave Ovamboland under any circumstances. So how can I get to Tsumeb?'

'This is something we'll have to plan carefully,' Mwatale said.

'Someone must go to Oshikango and get a pass for you.'

'But who?' I replied. 'It is very dangerous forging a pass.' After some discussion my brother, Alexander, volunteered. He wasn't a SWAPO cadre; he had just come along with me to the meeting. As brothers we always went places together. He had recently came back from contract in Tsumeb and could tell the Native Commissioner that he wanted to get some things he'd left there. This was agreed to by the other comrades.

We also drew up a strategy for approaching the UN Committee; what to tell them and so on. The first thing we wanted to do was urge the UN to take over control of Namibia, since the territory was the UN's responsibility and didn't belong to South Africa. We would ask the UN representatives to put pressure on all member nations to force South Africa out of our country. We also wanted the UN to examine our situation — the contract-labour system, the pass laws, and all the other forms of oppression felt by every Namibian. The comrades told me to be very specific about this point to the Committee.

Two days later Alexander went to Oshikango. He told the clerk in the Native Commissioner's office about wanting to pick up his things in Tsumeb and wasn't questioned at all; they knew he had worked at Tsumeb for many years. So he got the travel pass and brought it to me. It was valid for one month and had the name Alexander Hamufenu Ndadi on it.

I borrowed Issaschar's bicycle and set out for Ondangua. On the way, just as I was near the border separating Ondangua district from Oukwanyama, a Land Rover pulled up beside me. It was van Beuren, a Boer who worked at the post office. He always said he was sympathetic to our cause; that he supported SWAPO. Once he even asked me for a membership card.

He stopped, 'Ndadi,' he yelled, 'where are you going?'

'I'm heading for Ondangua.'

'It's a long way. Throw your bike in the back, I'll give you a lift.' I was tired and accepted. We reached Ondangua early in the evening. 'Where are you off to now?' he asked.

'I'm going over to ja Toivo's place.'

'Oh, really?' he said. 'I see him now and again. Haven't seen him lately, but I think he's still around. Good luck.'

I found ja Toivo at home. He was happy to see me. 'Well? What happened? Did you get the pass?'

'Yes, Alex got it for me,' I said, showing him my pass. 'It was no problem. I'm on my way.'

'I hear the Committee is now in Salisbury* ,' he said. 'From there they'll go to Bechuana† , then most likely to Rundu, then on to Grootfontein and Tsumeb. So you'd better get there soon.'

I slept at ja Toivo's and caught the bus for Tsumeb in the morning. I ran into van Beuren again and we talked shortly before I boarded the bus. The bus ride took most of the day and it was getting dark as we pulled into Tsumeb. There I met Issaschar's friend, Paulus Haita. He was surprised to see me and offered to put me up at his house.

Paulus is a really nice fellow; he gave me everything I needed. I washed and put on some clothes he gave me. Then he showed me a separate room where I could rest. I asked him to go tell my brothers, Hamutenya and Issaschar, that I was in town. It was late, but Paulus went on his bicycle to the mine compound. Soon he returned with Hamutenya. Issaschar came later; someone else told him I was there. We talked and next morning I went into downtown and bought a newspaper. The headlines read: 'Fabregat Committee Refused Entry.' It really hit me. The Committee was not coming!

Just then I ran into van Beuren again. 'What a surprise!' he said.

'Hello,' I said. 'What are you doing here?'

'You know I work for the post office. They sent me down to clear up a few things . . . When did you get in?'

I didn't answer. By now I was getting a little suspicious. It almost seemed he was following me around. 'Did you hear the UN Committee was refused entry?' he asked. 'I hear they've already returned to the UN. They got as far as Salisbury, but were threatened with arrest by Eric Louw‡ if they landed in Namibia.'

'I've just read about it — too bad.'

'Yes, what a pity. I really wanted these people to come and see what South Africa is doing here.'

* In Southern Rhodesia, now Harare

† Bechuanaland, now Botswana

‡ South African Foreign Minister

I was now almost convinced that van Beuren was a police spy. First, he comes out of nowhere to give me a lift. Then I see him at the Ondangua bus station. And now I meet him here . . . and he always comes on with sympathy for Namibians. I said goodbye and left, saying I had to go and meet my brothers. Later we discovered that van Beuren really was employed by Special Branch. He had been assigned to keep track of me.

I found Hamutenya and Issaschar behind the compound, where the men gathered after work to talk and drink *tombo*, homemade beer. Many of the workers were excited to meet me and wanted to learn what I'd been doing as a SWAPO organiser. As we talked, some police arrived — two Whites and three Africans, led by Sergeant Ellis. They were all Special Branch and had attended many of our meetings. The Sergeant came straight up to me. 'Where's your pass?'

I knew I was in trouble. I handed him Alexander's pass.

'Is this *your* pass?'

'Yes.'

He just laughed. 'Yes. You're the one we want. Come along and don't try any tricks.'

They took me to McClelland, the compound manager, and told him they'd found me around the compound without a proper pass. McClelland didn't seem to care. Said he was busy and just ignored them. Sgt Ellis then made it clear that I wasn't there just to drink beer; I was a dangerous Ovambo agitator.

McClelland still looked bored. He asked me some questions, walked around the room, and finally said, 'Since this Ovambo's not working here, he's none of my business. Do what you want with him. Just leave me alone!'

The angry sergeant then drove me to the charge office. A South African Police officer and two Black Special Branch agents were waiting for us. I was charged with breaking restriction orders and entering Tsumeb illegally.

'But I've got a pass,' I protested.

'Don't press your luck, *donner*; we know your tricks.'

There wasn't much I could say; being in the hands of these fascists was no joke.

I was searched and they took everything out of my pockets: pens, my watch and a few worthless papers. I knew better than to carry important papers on me. Then they wrote out a report and locked me up. The Tsumeb police station had five cells: one for White women, one for African women, one for White men and two for African men. The cell was just like others I'd been in. As usual, there was a high wall surrounding an open compound where prisoners ate. Each cell opened into the compound. I was alone in my cell. The place was really stinking. The slopping-out pot was full and everything was filthy. I could hardly breathe. Sitting on the cement floor, my spirits were pretty low.

In the evening they brought me some cold maize porridge and beans. I wasn't hungry and ate very little. It was now winter and becoming very cold. Namibia's May, June and July are cold and windy. In the concrete cell I had only two thin blankets full of lice. I put one on the floor and I used the other to cover myself. It was so cold I could hardly move. I stayed in the same position all night — everywhere else I turned was like ice.

In the morning an African constable who knew my brothers came to see me. They had sent him to find out what I was charged with; maybe they could get me a lawyer or raise money for my fine. I said I didn't know if there'd be a trial or if they'd just hold me indefinitely.

'But why are you being kept alone,' he wondered. Apparently, I was in the cell for women; they didn't want me to mix with the other prisoners.

'Are you a SWAPO man?' he asked.

I looked at him. 'Yes, I am.'

'I see. So you're involved in politics. Now I know why.' He turned and left.

The following day I was taken to the Special Branch office. Sergeant Boois, a South African, was there. He asked why I'd come to Tsumeb and if I'd already met with the Fabregat Committee.

'Who told you I came here to see the Fabregat Committee?'

'We know everything about you. So don't give us any nonsense. You hear! You're in trouble and you better be good, help yourself out. We'll show you that what you're attempting can't succeed. It'll just bring you misery — and everyone else involved too. You have a real problem Kaffir! You were restricted to Ovamboland and you left illegally, using your brother's name.'

'It doesn't matter,' I said. 'I've been in trouble so many times with you South Africans that it hardly bothers me any more.'

'But this time your problem is serious! Holding SWAPO meetings, well, we know the pack of lies you're telling. But going to Oshikango and forging a pass is a very serious crime.' He grinned. 'You'll see what happens . . .'

A Special Branch officer came in. 'What is going on?' he asked.

'This is *Mr* Vinnia Ndadi,' said Boois, 'one of our black agitators. He talks a lot and writes letters all over the world, trying to get the Ovambos to revolt. He's restricted to Ovamboland but came to Tsumeb on his brother's pass.'

'Let me talk to him,' said Kastner, the Special Branch man.

I was taken into another office. First he asked me why I'd come to Tsumeb. 'To see my brothers,' I said. He asked me their names, where they worked. I told him.

'Look here,' he said, 'you're full of shit. We know you came here to meet that UN Committee.'

'I don't know what you're talking about,' I said.

'Listen,' Kastner barked, 'I know of your OPO work in Walvis Bay! That you tried to stow away and go to the UN! You were deported, have been working for SWAPO in Ovamboland, and came here to see this UN Committee. Now why the hell don't you cut out the bullshit?' His face got very red. Then he sat back and lit a cigarette.

'Do yourself a favour. If you co-operate you won't be detained.'

'But I'm not guilty,' I replied calmly.

'OK you bastard! If that's what you want you'll get it.'

I was kept in my cell for a week, in complete isolation.

One day, as I was lying on my back staring at the ceiling, the door was flung open and a Black policeman stepped in. 'Get out!' he shouted. They were holding a woman who had been arrested in the location. They pushed her inside and the door was closed. I was taken to one of the men's cells. It contained twelve prisoners, was about fifteen by fifteen feet and stank to high heaven. The air was so hot and close I could hardly breathe.

An old friend was there — Philip Namholo. He was Ovambo and worked in Tsumeb as a clerk. They hadn't told him why he'd been arrested. We had plenty of time to talk about developments at home, what SWAPO was doing, and so on. We had to be careful, however, since a police agent may have been placed in the cell.

I was held incommunicado, as they call it, for three months. Nobody was allowed to visit me and I couldn't write or receive letters. Then one afternoon two Special Branch men came and took me to the charge office. They said I was released, then re-arrested me. They often do this in order to hold prisoners without a charge. I was to be returned to Ovamboland under police escort. I got back my belongings and left in a police van with Sergeant Stengel, a German in the South African Police Force. We left Tsumeb at 2 p.m. and reached Ondangua around 8. We drove straight to a South African Army base where I was turned over to a group of soldiers while Stengel went to see the camp commander. Some of the soldiers were drunk and started abusing me. I must have looked in bad shape with my full beard and the effects of three months in Tsumeb. The soldiers called me names like 'Bloody Lumumba,' shouted stupidities like 'Here's Haile Selassie,' 'A damn Black Nasser,' etc. Then one of the drunk soldiers got an idea: 'This dangerous bastard shouldn't be left out like this! Better lock him up in a lorry.'

An officer came over at that moment and told them to stop fooling around with me. 'This Kaffir was brought here by the Tsumeb police, so knock it off!' They started up on me again, however, as soon as the officer left. I was forced into a tent and pushed down; they were swearing and cursing as they searched me and took my knife and the few shillings I had. They were all White, of course. No Blacks were taken into the South African Army at that time.

I was getting worried about what they might do, when the officer returned. He called me outside and took me to a captain who asked some questions. Did I belong to SWAPO? What was my position? What was I doing in Tsumeb? Etc., etc.

'Yes,' I said. 'I'm a SWAPO organiser in Ovamboland. I was visiting my brothers in . . . .' 'How do you organise people?' he interrupted. I didn't lie, just gave him very brief answers. They had many documents about my activities so he must have known my story well.

When the questioning was over he said, 'You'll sleep here tonight, and tomorrow I'll take you home.'

I could hardly believe it. But he went on: 'You're a free man now;

here's a blanket, so sleep near the fire.' A fire was burning nearby where they kept a pot of water for coffee boiling all the time.

Early in the morning some South Africans woke me to wash their dishes. I was getting started when the captain came over with two of his men. 'Who told you to wash these dishes?' he asked. 'Never mind! Get your stuff; you're leaving.'

I put my things into a Land Rover and was driven to Ondangua by two soldiers. I waited in the lorry as they went to see the Native Commissioner. Soon they came out and we took off again. Before reaching Omafo I asked them to stop. I didn't want to go to Oshikango. I'd heard that Strydom was handing Namibian 'agitators' over to the Portuguese, saying they were Angolans. The Portuguese would then send them off to some island as slave labourers.

'But the Native Commissioner wants to see you.'

'Yes, I know. But I can't go now . . . . Not today, anyway. I'll go and report to him soon, but first I must go home. I've been away over three months.' They looked at each other, talked about it awhile, then said, 'OK, get out.'

I walked the rest of the way home. My family knew I'd been in prison — I think my brothers had written — and they were very happy to see me. My mother said I had got very thin; skinny in fact. But she'd fatten me up again. It took some time for me to recover my full strength.

I'd been home a week when Kaxumba came. I told him what had happened. He said there would be a meeting of the branch executive the next evening in the house of a new member, John Kemanye, in Okalongo. Then he left.

At the meeting I reported what had happened to me. The others talked of developments in Ovamboland during my absence — of meetings, efforts at mobilising the people, and so on. More and more people were joining SWAPO all the time. Every region of Ovamboland was represented at our meeting and many questions were asked about my experience in gaol. We talked late into the night.

During the period at home I fell in love with a girl at Engela Girls' School. Her name was Sarah. We first met in 1960 when I returned from Walvis Bay. She lived fifteen miles away and I would either walk or take my brother's bike to go and visit her. Soon after we met,

I told her I wanted to get married. She didn't give me a definite answer; said she wasn't sure she'd be allowed to marry so young. But we agreed to go on meeting until she was able to marry. My brother had spoken with her family on my behalf.

After returning from Tsumeb I went to visit Sarah and discuss our plans. She was really scared, however, because her family said I was a communist; didn't want her to see me again. And the principal at Engela told her she'd better not get involved with politics. She was afraid he would expel her from school.

'Dear Sarah,' I said, 'I don't want you to get expelled. It's better if you continue school. But I can't give up my work with SWAPO. Some day — soon perhaps — Namibia will become independent; then we'll talk again and decide what to do.'

I never went to see her again. She continued school and I did my best to forget her — though to tell the truth, I was quite depressed for several months. This was in September 1961. In May the following year another UN Committee was formed; this time led by a diplomat from the Philippines named Carpio. It was scheduled to come to Namibia via South Africa; first to Windhoek, then to Ovamboland. I heard this news on the radio not long before the Committee was due to arrive. I went immediately to Ohalushu.

At Kaukungua's house I found two comrades from Ongandjera. We decided to go straight to Ondangua, where the Committee would sit the following day. We left in the evening and cycled all night without stopping. At 7 a.m. we reached Andimba Toivo ja Toivo's place. There we found people from all over. They were already busy with placards. Everybody sat down to discuss how we could best approach Carpio. A group consisting of myself, ja Toivo, Kaxumba, Simon Kaukungua, Lameck Ithete and Nathaniel Homateni from Okalongo was chosen to go and try to meet with the UN Committee.

At the administrative centre a huge crowd joined us, singing freedom songs and waving placards. Some chiefs and headmen were also there, ordered by government to testify on behalf of South Africa. Carpio, however, wasn't there. The police said he'd gone to Okatana to see a new missionary hospital. We didn't know whether to believe them. Wanting to make sure, Lameck Ithete and I asked a local SWAPO member with a lorry to drive us to Okatana. There we found the Carpio Committee being escorted by the Chief Native

Commissioner from Windhoek, Mr Blignaut, and some other South Africans. When they left, we followed and reached Ondangua at the same time.

The crowd was still singing freedom songs. We joined them. People were then called in separately to see Carpio. Chief Ushona from Ongandjera was called in first. We were given a copy of his statement. He said, basically, that he was quite happy with the South African administration in our country; that contract labourers from his area seemed to be treated well, but that he, being a chief, didn't know exactly what was happening. He only knew that he received gifts or money from the workers when they returned from contract. Otherwise, he knew nothing. Other chiefs and headmen were then called in. They didn't give us statements, so I don't know what they told the Committee.

Finally, SWAPO was called in. The Boers raised no objections; government had agreed that the Committee was free to go anywhere and see anyone they wanted. First we were introduced to Carpio, the vice-chairman, d'Alva, from Mexico, a secretary named Yarrow and another whose name I can't remember. Carpio said we were free to speak our minds.

Ja Toivo spoke first. He talked about the contract labour system, repressive pass laws, police raids on houses at night, the restriction of Namibian leaders and gaoling without charge of those opposed to *apartheid*. Carpio turned to the Chief Native Commissioner, Blignaut, who denied everything. They wanted more specifics, so I started explaining exactly how the contract system worked, how men were recruited by SWANLA, taken to the camp in Grootfontein and bought by whoever wanted workers. In all, we spent more than three hours with the Committee.

When the meeting was over they assured us they would take all the information they had gathered back to the UN, where it would be discussed and published as documentary evidence. We expressed our hope and confidence in them, then asked Carpio to talk to the huge crowd outside. He said it wasn't proper; he was authorised only to talk with SWAPO officials. We insisted: 'The people want to see you. You can just introduce the Committee to them, you don't have to make a statement.'

Finally he agreed and went outside where the crowd had been

111

waiting many hours. He told them he had the cooperation of the South African government and was thus able to come as far as Ovamboland. A question then rang out from the crowd. 'Is it true that the UN is going to free the Namibian people from the Boers?' Yes, said Carpio; the UN hoped to be able to do this. The Committee left for Windhoek immediately after our meeting. We went to ja Toivo's place where we talked and rested. None of us had slept the night before so we were extremely tired.

A few weeks after the Carpio visit, Blignaut announced in Windhoek that SWAPO members were no longer banned from employment outside Ovamboland* . When I heard this I wrote to Tsumeb Corporation and, to my surprise, got a reply by telegram that they had a job for me. Sending an application by post was fairly common among educated people when they wanted to work for a particular company, but this was the first time I'd tried it. The telegram was signed by the compound manager.

In Ondangua I went to the SWANLA office and showed them the telegram. This time I didn't have to wait. I got an 'A' classification right away and was told I would leave the following day. That evening I went to see ja Toivo and we had a long discussion. I told him I was going to Tsumeb to work, but that I would also do SWAPO work there. 'OK brother,' he said, 'as long as you continue working for our people. The rest of us will remain in Ovamboland.'

In Tsumeb I went straight to the compound manager and showed him the telegram. He didn't seem to remember my application. 'Good,' he said with some hesitation, 'we need clerks, but first we'll have to give you a test.'

It was simple and I passed easily. Then he sent me to the Native Affairs division where I was interviewed by a man in charge of new recruits. I told him about my work in the SWANLA office in Grootfontein and that I could both read and write Afrikaans. That did the trick. 'Good,' he said, 'real good! You'll be useful, no doubt about it. Go back to the compound and we'll call you.'

Then one, two, three days passed, but still I heard nothing. I did learn that Sergeant Boois had been to the Native Affairs office and told them about my activities and record with Special Branch. When

---

* A measure introduced to restrict SWAPO members

I finally got called in, the personnel officer had completely changed.

'Look,' he said, 'I thought we might give you a job here in the office. But that's not possible now. We can't risk hiring trouble-makers. You'd best leave now.' I don't know if he was scared or angry, but his face was flushed and his breathing short.

I went to see the compound manager and told him what happened. He looked worried, saying, 'I can't do a thing about it. I don't assign jobs around here, Native Affairs does. If they won't take you, there's nothing I can do. You'll have to stick around and accept whatever job comes up.'

Another two weeks passed. I continued living in the compound. Then one morning I was called to the timber yard, where they cut wood for the whole Tsumeb operation — props to hold the rock in place down in the mines, building materials, firewood, etc. I was given a job at one pound ten a week.

I would remain at this job for almost a year. Work began at 7 a.m. and we quit at 5. There was no lunch break. We ate breakfast in the compound; sour porridge, mealie bread and black coffee — it was often so bad I couldn't eat it. We got our food at the kitchen and took it to our rooms, each about fourteen feet square with concrete tables and concrete bunks for sixteen men. We had to keep our room clean, scrubbing it down on Sundays, our only day off.

Most of the men worked underground in the mine. Others had outside jobs like watering the parks, working as houseboys for the Whites, or in the mine hotels. The entire town was — and still is — run by Tsumeb Corporation; from the mines, power plant and water supply, to the parks and hotels. More than 4,000 workers lived in one huge compound. It had a high wall and only one gate, guarded by police.

I was elected chairman of the newly formed SWAPO branch soon after I arrived. OPO had been active at Tsumeb for some time and I knew many of the Ovambo contract workers. The chairman had just finished his contract and I was elected to replace him. About twenty people attended the branch executive meeting — ten from the Tsumeb Women's Council. Old Levi Mwashekele, the organising secretary, chaired the meeting. Albert Nazab was elected vice-chairman.

Soon after, I got permission from Rottenbach, the location

superintendent, to hold a rally. We made posters and stuck them on trees — one in the compound and two or three in the location was enough for everybody to learn about the meeting.

More than 5,000 people turned out on a Saturday evening after work. There were three speakers: Nazab, Shikua and me. The Special Branch came too, led by Sergeant Boois with his tape recorder. At this time the case of Namibia was before the International Court of Justice at The Hague. In my speech I explained this to the people and told them what it meant. Others talked about SWAPO and the importance of achieving unity among all Namibians. There were no incidents; everything went smoothly from beginning to end.

Afterwards Boois came over and said he would check our speeches closely. We might be summoned to the station, he said, and charged with 'inciting to violence' or riot. We had known what he was after, however, and were careful to avoid 'dangerous' statements in our speeches. The people knew what we meant and could read between the lines.

At another meeting, about a month later, a SWAPO leader from Windhoek, John ya Otto, came to speak to the workers. The crowd was even bigger than before since the speaker was our acting secretary general from SWAPO headquarters. We met in a grove of trees to avoid the hot sun. I made a brief opening speech and introduced John ya Otto. He talked about the need for unity among Namibians and of the work SWAPO was doing in Windhoek. He thanked the people of Tsumeb for their contribution to the struggle for freedom and independence. He also said that Sam Nujoma was presenting our case at the UN in New York, but that there was little hope the UN would free Namibia. 'We must understand this!' he said. 'It will be up to us to liberate ourselves. No one will do it for us.' The workers clapped loudly. They knew what he meant. Special Branch was there again with their tape recorder and no doubt had many spies scattered in the crowd.

Disappointment with the UN effort was widespread by this time . . . and peaceful means against the fascist South African regime had proved useless. Some of our members were already receiving military training; but this was a secret only a few of us knew about.

A few weeks after this meeting I went to McClelland and asked to be transferred. He said, 'You know damned well I didn't send you to the timber yard; the Native Affairs Office did. They don't want you, because you hate Boers.' McClelland was from Canada and spoke English to me — though he could also speak Afrikaans.

'I don't hate Boers,' I protested. 'What I hate is oppression, and you know damn well that Namibians are being oppressed by the South African government. That's the truth, and I don't hide it. I tell the people exactly what the Boers are doing in Namibia. I don't hate Boers because they're Boers; I hate them only because they are oppressing us.'

'Listen, Ndadi, I'm not a politician . . . not even interested in politics. That's your business. Anyway, I'll see what I can do for you.'

It was winter and very cold, and my job was really terrible . . . and heavy. Nevertheless, I continued, waiting for word from the compound manager.

Nothing happened for a long time. Issaschar and Hamutenya, who were still working as clerks, finally went to see McClelland, asking about my transfer. He told them what he'd told me. 'You know what your brother's up to. The company doesn't want him here at all. They'd like him to break his contract and return to Ovamboland. If he gets an office job, he may never leave. It's not good that the police come regularly to check on him. But, as I told him, I'll try to get him a transfer.'

Finally, one day in June 1963, Native Affairs called me in. They'd been requested by McClelland to find me another job. I was to be transferred to the lamp room where mine workers got their head lamps charged between shifts. My job was to do the recharging, replace broken parts, and so on.

A month or so after I had started the new job I got news that Maxwilili, now SWAPO acting vice-president, was coming up from Walvis Bay with Frank Abrams and Valentine Katumbe. They wanted us to arrange a mass meeting in Tsumeb. I put in for a permit but this time my application was turned down. No explanation — just rejected. The letters from the superintendent's office just said, 'Sorry, your application has been rejected. The meeting cannot take place.' It was the first time we had been refused permission for a public meeting.

Maxwilili and the others came anyway. We met in the evening, soon after they arrived and I told Maxwilili the bad news.

'How many times did you apply?' he asked.

'Three,' and I handed him copies of our applications and the letters. 'And they gave no reason.'

'According to the law,' he said, 'any legal organisation can hold public meetings as long as it applies for a permit — even if the application is turned down. We cannot leave Tsumeb without having addressed the people.'

I was hesitant. 'This isn't Walvis Bay, you know; the Boers here are really vicious. If we go ahead, we're almost sure to be arrested.'

But Maxwilili was insistent. 'I don't care. They can arrest, but we have to hold a meeting.'

We put up posters and on Saturday at 1 o'clock there was a huge crowd at the meeting place. We didn't use microphones or bullhorns at meetings, we just stood on tables and shouted.

I was introducing the comrades from Walvis Bay when three police cars pulled up. They parked some distance away; I could see they were armed with machine guns. I instructed the people to listen closely to what our vice-president had to say.

Just then Sergeant Boois and a group of South African Police came over and ordered us into a car — Maxwilili, Martin Shailemo and I. We were going to be taken to the police station. The crowd, however, was furious. They closed in on the car, as Boois was trying to turn, and surrounded it completely. It was a small Volkswagen and they shook it and pounded on the roof.

'Look, Sergeant Boois,' Maxwilili said, 'you're making a big mistake. If you're not careful there's going to be a riot. We don't want any bloodshed, but the situation may get beyond our control. Why don't you just let us go on with the meeting? You can arrest us afterwards . . .'

Boois was obviously shaken. The crowd was pounding and shouting. 'You must let our leaders speak! If you take them to prison we'll break them out,' and so forth. This clearly frightened him. He paused, then said, 'Go and finish your meeting.'

After the rally we went to Levi Mwashekele's place and reviewed the situation. We knew we'd be summoned to court, so decided to

get a lawyer from Windhoek. Maxwilili and the others left immediately for Walvis Bay.

A week later police came to the lamp room with a summons for me
signed by the magistrate. I was to appear before him on 14 July at
10 a.m. Old Mwashekele and Matias Kanana were also summonsed,
as were Maxwilili and Frank Abrams in Walvis Bay. The latter
arrived a day before our case was due. We had a meeting in the
evening and discussed bringing a lawyer in from Windhoek. The
question was really about money. Tsumeb branch had about £500.
'OK, that's enough for a good lawyer,' Maxwilili decided. 'We can
even bring him here by plane.'

Next morning we went to court. The magistrate first called the
prosecutor to explain the charge. 'The defendants organised an
illegal meeting on 27 June in Tsumeb municipality,' the attorney
started. 'They had been refused permission by the location superintendent, and are therefore guilty of . . .' He quoted a number of
articles and clauses from his fascist law books related to contraven-
ing South African laws prohibiting unauthorised political meetings.
We, on our hand, pleaded not guilty and told the magistrate we had
got a lawyer to defend us.

'Where is your lawyer?' he asked.

'He will be coming from Windhoek today. We ask that the case be
postponed until tomorrow, when he will have arrived and studied
the charges.'

He reluctantly agreed, saying, 'He'd better be here at 10 sharp,
when the court will begin its session; the trial will proceed with or
without a defence lawyer.'

From the courthouse we went straight to the Tsumeb Lawyers'
Association. We told the man in charge we would be likely to go to
prison if we didn't get a good attorney before 10 the next morning.
'We want O'Linn from Windhoek to take our case. Can you get in
touch with him?'

'I'll telephone him right now. But tell me, can you pay his plane
fare up here? It's £100 by charter, you know.' We assured him we
had the money.

O'Linn had defended SWAPO people in Windhoek several times.
He was White, of course; there were no African lawyers in Namibia.
He immediately agreed to take our case and assured us he'd be there

on time. At 9 the following morning we went to the Lawyers' Association office. O'Linn didn't arrive, however, till a quarter to ten, so we had to quickly explain our situation to him.

'Do you have copies of all your applications?'

'Sure, here they are,' I said.

He went through them. 'All right, we'd better get over to the court house. This is all I'll need.'

What a fine lawyer he was. He knew exactly what to do from the moment we rushed into the court room . . . and we made it just in time. As soon as we entered, the magistrate called our names. We entered the dock and the proceedings started. First, the prosecutor repeated his charges and we pleaded not guilty. Then O'Linn stood up. 'I would like to know exactly how this meeting can be declared illegal?' he asked the magistrate. 'Didn't my clients apply for a permit?'

The magistrate didn't know and asked the prosecutor, who also didn't know.

O'Linn went on: 'I know the defendants made three written requests to the location superintendent. Here are copies of their applications' — he waved them in the air before handing them to the magistrate. 'This meeting wasn't illegal at all! My clients made three official requests. I would like to know who refused these quite proper applications for a public meeting.'

'Mr Rottenbach, the superintendent, was on leave. His secretary was in charge.'

She was called to the witness box and O'Linn asked her name.

'Maria Katrina, when you were in the office during this period of Mr Rottenbach's leave did you receive any letters from the SWAPO office here in Tsumeb?'

'Yes, I received three letters from SWAPO.'

'What were they about?'

'They requested Mr Rottenbach to authorise a SWAPO meeting in the location.'

'What did you do with these letters?'

'Well, since Mr Rottenbach was away, I turned down the requests.'

'Why?'

'I feared there might be a riot or something; you know these things often happen . . . and I didn't want to be responsible.'

'How many SWAPO meetings have there been in Tsumeb?'

'Oh, several, I think.'

'Was there ever any violence reported at these meetings?'

'No, not that I know of . . . .'

'Then why did you think the meeting requested would result in a riot?'

She couldn't answer; just shrugged and said she didn't want the responsibility on her head. She was very uncomfortable.

'So, you replied to all three of these letters with simple rejections. Did it ever occur to you to ask why the defendants were so persistent about holding this meeting?'

'No, it didn't.'

'I see. And you didn't call in any SWAPO leader to ask why they wanted this meeting so badly?'

'No, I didn't.'

'Very well. Now where is your authorisation from Mr Rottenbach giving you the power to make such decisions? Have you got a letter or something?'

'Yes; it's . . . it's in the office.'

O'Linn requested that the letter be brought to the court and the magistrate agreed. There was a break while Maria Katrina went to her office. Apparently, there wasn't any letter — so she forged one. O'Linn must have suspected it. When the court reconvened, he took just one look at it and smiled. 'Oh, very good.' He gave it to the court clerk. Then he wound up the defence, turning to the magistrate: 'There was nobody left officially in charge of Mr Rottenbach's job. This letter proves nothing, and besides I believe it is a forgery. Therefore, the refusal of SWAPO to hold the meeting in question was invalid and I ask that the case be dismissed.' He sat down.

The magistrate had been taking notes. Now he had to make a decision. 'Well,' he said, 'the defendants did get a reply from the office of the superintendent, though Mr Rottenbach himself wasn't there. Therefore, they shouldn't have held their meeting. On the other hand, since the secretary has failed to convince the court that she was formally authorised to handle such requests, the meeting was not officially prohibited. Thus the accused are not guilty.' He then turned to us. 'You are free to go.'

It was a good feeling to walk out of that courtroom free. I was really impressed with O'Linn. 'If we always had lawyers like that, many fewer SWAPO members would be in gaol now,' I thought.

Special Branch was furious we'd been let off, but there was nothing they could do about it. Encouraged by our victory, we went on holding meetings. The police never again tried to break them up so long as I was in Tsumeb. They did, however, keep a close check on us and always attended our rallies.

The Tsumeb branch grew rapidly, as did the Women's Council. Many women joined during this period. Whenever a meeting was scheduled they would inform all the members. Sometimes they organised picnics where they'd sell homemade cakes, sausage and soft drinks to raise money for SWAPO. I continued as branch chairman . . . and there was always a Special Branch tail on me.

After the case our lamp room foreman, a very stupid Boer named Conradie, started getting at me. One day he came over as I worked on a lamp. 'I don't understand you, Kaffir; the bloody police is always after you. What are you up to anyway?' He hadn't known at first that I was in SWAPO; maybe he didn't even know what SWAPO was. But when I was summonsed to court the police had come and told him they wanted me. After that he always tried to intimidate me and make things difficult. I just ignored him.

There were three shifts in the lamp room: 8 a.m. to 4 p.m.; 4 till 12, and a night shift from midnight to 8 a.m. There were two of us, plus a foreman, on each shift and always plenty of work. Batteries had to be charged between shifts and regularly filled with acid; lamps always had to be repaired. My wage was the same as before, one pound ten.

7 Exile

On 22 June 1964 my contract expired. I left Tsumeb with my brother Issaschar that very day. His contract had expired a month before but he waited for me. Before leaving I called a meeting of the branch executive and suggested that Albert Nazab take over the chairmanship. This was unanimously agreed upon.

We caught a bus for Ondangua where I went to see ja Toivo. He told me many SWAPO members had been arrested and beaten. A few had already left the country, headed for Tanganyika.

This is what had happened: de Wet Nel, South African Minister of Native Affairs, had come to Ohangwena to tell the people of government's intention to divide Namibia into so-called *bantustans*. The Boers planned to create many of these in Namibia and South Africa. Each separate tribe would be given a 'homeland' — the Damara would get their 'homeland,' the Hereros theirs, the Ovambos theirs, and so on for the Okavangos, Caprivians, etc. These were the plans that de Wet Nel disclosed at Ohangwena in March 1964.

Simon Kaukungua, Kaxumba and several other SWAPO officers stood up after de Wet Nel's speech and said they were totally opposed to the creation of *bantustans* in Namibia; that it was ridiculous for a South African to come to Namibia and say such things. They also said no Namibians wanted their country divided; they wanted an independent and united Namibia.

You can imagine, this was very heavy stuff for such a meeting. Just as Kaukungua finished speaking, the local headman, Elia Weyulu — a true stooge of the Boers if ever there was one — got up and pointed his gun at Kaukungua. He might have fired, but women grabbed the gun away from him. Our women were very well organised; most people fear guns but the women acted decisively and probably saved Kaukungua's life. Nothing more happened then, but

Strydom made it clear that anyone opposing the South African plan could be dealt with severely.

Soon after this incident, Strydom sent police to Kaukungua's house to bring him in — dead or alive. SWAPO was growing fast now and becoming a real threat.

Kaukungua heard the police were coming for him and hid in the forest. Later he decided to leave the country; it was useless at that time to remain, since public meetings had been banned and we had no other means of struggle.

As ja Toivo told me this he seemed somewhat discouraged. 'So what can we do? We can't have meetings . . . can't even talk to anybody there are so many informers around. What do you think you should do, Vinnia?'

I thought for a moment. There was much that needed doing in Ovamboland, but conditions were becoming impossible. My brother Hamutenya had already left the country with Kaukungua, as had many other SWAPO members. Most of them went to Francis-town in Botswana, and from there to Dar es Salaam. 'Maybe it's best if I leave, too,' I said finally. 'After all, it's better to work outside than be shot here, or rot away in some Boer prison.'

Ja Toivo agreed and wished me luck.

I found Issaschar in town and we took lorries, first to Omafo, then home to Ouhongo. We got in late that evening.

Next day my father slaughtered a goat to celebrate our homecoming. Everybody was happy to have us back. They told us of the incident at Ohangwena and what was happening in Ovamboland. They pleaded with me to be more careful now that the headmen were free to kill SWAPO leaders at will. The situation, they said, was very dangerous and they warned against my trying to call any meetings. I told them about my talk with ja Toivo and of my decision to leave Namibia. 'I can work outside,' I said, 'and I might even get a scholarship to continue my education.' They didn't like the idea of my leaving; but on the other hand they feared what would happen if I stayed. So they agreed finally.

'Maybe it's the only thing to do . . .' my father sighed; 'better than getting arrested or killed here.'

Matias Kanana from Onambutu, who had been in Tsumeb with me, also wanted to go. I spent a couple of weeks at home preparing for the journey and working with my father and Issaschar. The days passed quickly and soon time came to say goodbye to my parents and Issaschar. It wasn't easy. I didn't know what would happen, whether I would ever come back to see them again. I just kept telling myself, 'Well, what else can I do? I have no real alternative.' My mother cried as we parted.

On my way to Onambutu, I stopped by Hamutenya's house and spoke with his wife. I said I was going to attend the wedding of an old friend. She didn't believe me. 'You're going to Tanganyika like your brother, I know.'

'No,' I said, 'you're wrong.' But she just laughed.

Kanana had been expecting me. He slaughtered a goat for our trip. We ate as much as we could and then packed the rest. I only took two spare shirts and a couple of thin blankets. I got everything into a small bag.

We just started walking straight east, through the jungle towards Okavango. It took two weeks to get to Rundu, the administrative centre of Okavango territory. We walked every day from dawn till sunset. In the jungle it's difficult to walk at night because of the wild animals. We passed through some villages where we bought food, but never let anyone know we were SWAPO members. The police were already patrolling the Okavango, knowing SWAPO militants were taking this route out of Namibia. When people asked where we were headed, we told them there was a Winela (Witwatersrand Native Labour Association) recruiting station which supplied workers to South African mines. Winela recruited mostly for the Rand mines. We were planning to get to Francistown, where there was a SWAPO camp, but to get there we had to become Winela recruits. Their trucks went from Rundu to Francistown, from where recruits were flown to Johannesburg. We had planned to get to Francistown, then run away.

We slept in the compound that night and early next morning we went to the Winela station. As we stood in the long queue of job seekers, three Special Branch men arrived. Fortunately, none of them knew me. Moving down the line, they asked everybody for identification and those who didn't have any were taken to their Land Rover for questioning. I suspected they were looking mainly for SWAPO members trying to flee the country.

My turn came and I told them I didn't have a card.

'OK, go over to the car!'

I walked slowly and just as the Black policeman opened the door — whoom — I took off. I'm sure I've never run so fast in my life . . . heading straight for the forest some hundred yards away. Two of the officers were right behind me, but I managed to lose them once I got into the bush. Then I lay flat and listened for their footsteps for several minutes. Nothing. They must have returned, thinking they'd get me later.

I had left my shoes at the Winela office and my bag was still in the compound. It contained some important things, like all my money, so I decided to go and get it despite the risk.

A policeman was at the gate. It was now almost dark. I walked quietly till I got close, then slipped quickly past him, ran to get my bag and continued to the far side of the compound. There I threw my bag over the fence and climbed over myself. It was high with barbed wire on top and getting over was very painful, especially without shoes. Still, it was better than being captured.

Once clear of the compound, I ran without stopping till I reached the river. Rundu is near the Okavango River, which borders Angola.

I walked along the bank for a mile or so, staying close to the forest. Then I met a young boy with a canoe. He agreed to take me across for one shilling.

On the other side was a big village. Hardly anybody spoke Oshikwanyama but the people were very friendly. They gave me homemade beer and something to eat. Later, three Ovakwanyama came across from Rundu.

'So, you've made it,' they said on seeing me. 'They are still looking for you in the bush and along the river. Your friend, Kanana, has been arrested. Too bad.'

I was now alone. 'Well,' I thought, 'you've no choice but to continue. No going back now!'

I had no food, so I asked two of the Ovakwanyama to go and buy me a big bag of mealie meal at Rundu. I gave them three pounds. There were no shops on the Angolan side. They returned next day with a 250-lb bag. Since I was alone, however, I sold most to the villagers and kept only a small sack for myself.

During the next few days, groups of men heading for Katima

Mulilo in Eastern Caprivi gathered in the village. The Winela station at Rundu accepted only those who had worked in the mines before or got an 'A' classification. At Katima Mulilo, however, they accept both new recruits and men in the 'B' and 'C' categories. Thus, many who get turned down at Rundu go on to Katima Mulilo on foot. It is a long walk; through Angola, into Zambia, and then to the Caprivi Strip from the north.

I decided this would be the best thing for me to do. Some other Oukwanyama and a group of twenty-nine Angolans — mostly Ovimbundus — were also going. The day before we left I bought a goat which we slaughtered. I kept some of the meat and sold the rest to others in our group. The villagers bought the skin and head. If I hadn't been on my way, I would have kept it.

We left around 5 pm, when it was cool enough to move, everyone carrying his few belongings and food in a bag. Four of us Ovakwanyama put our food in a big bag which we took turns carrying. The others carried their own things separately. We walked from sunrise to sunset and on the third day crossed the Cuito River; then a week later, the Lumuna, and after two more weeks we reached the Luengue. Part of the way we walked through the nights too, because we were sometimes as much as a hundred miles between water holes or rivers. Many people in the past had died of thirst in this area. Other parts couldn't be crossed at night time because of lions.

At the Luengue River we ran completely out of food. I still had money left, but it didn't matter; money just wasn't known in this region. If you gave somebody a shilling he'd most likely put a hole through it and wear it round his neck. You could die with your pockets full of money. I managed to sell one of my blankets for a bucket of corn which we pounded to meal. Some village women helped us sift it.

Our group had no official leader, but as we went on I became more or less the leader since the others always respected my opinion and advice. Nobody knew my plans, they simply assumed I was going to work on the mines. I never once mentioned SWAPO.

Two weeks after Luengue we reached the Utembo River; then another two weeks or so to the Cuando where it crosses into Zambia. Before this time a disagreement had developed among us. We reached a fork in the road. Somebody said we should take the north fork but the Angolans wanted to take the southern route.

'No,' I said, 'we've been advised to take the left fork.'

But they wouldn't listen. 'You Ovakwanyama always confuse people,' one of them said. 'If you want to go left, go; we'll move south.'

So we parted company . . . the four of us heading north.

When we reached the Cuando we heard that the Angolans had beaten us by a day, but had unfortunately run into a Portuguese patrol which took them to the *chefe do posto* in the local administrative district. They were being held locked up in a Catholic church.

We hid in the forest until late evening. The Portuguese were thought to be even more brutal than the Boers. We were hungry and very tired, but it was necessary to stay in hiding. Later that night we went to a nearby village. There we boiled the rest of our mealie meal and ate it plain, without meat or relish. A villager promised to have a canoe ready for us the next day. Then we slept.

We returned to the forest before dawn and stayed until about 10, when a young man came and told us the canoe was ready. We set off immediately. At this point the Cuando River is very, very wide and the youth poled for several hours before we reached Sangombo on the Zambian side. I couldn't believe we were really in Zambia at last . . . don't think I could have walked another day.

There was a Winela station at Sangombo. Zambians wanting work in South Africa came here for transport to Katima Mulilo, where the real recruiting was done. We slept in the yard of the compound. The barracks were dirty and full of bugs. There was no food to be had.

About 3 a.m. I woke up suddenly. People were running around making all sorts of noise. My friends were already out of their blankets. 'What's happening?' I asked.

'Get up, Ndadi! Lions! There are lions here!'

The compound manager's pigs at the edge of the compound had been taken by the lions — one killed on the spot, its head completely severed, and another badly wounded around the throat and screaming fiercely. A third was gone altogether. No one had a gun. The manager drove up with his lorry and turned the headlights in the direction of the screams. The lions were still there — standing, staring into the lights, another lying down licking its paws.

Nobody went back to sleep. We made a big fire and sat around it till dawn. By then, the lions had left. And there was plenty of meat around. I joked, saying my father had sent me this meat because he knew I was very hungry. 'You see,' I said, 'my father belongs to the lion clan.' I didn't like pork, but I was starving and ate it with great pleasure. The manager sold most of the meat, but I got mine free because I helped him clean the carcasses.

Later that day in the village, I met a fellow called Tuta who was the UPA* representative in Sangombo. I told him I came from Namibia and was headed for Dar es Salaam. 'I'm trying to get transport to Lusaka; once there I can phone the SWAPO office in Dar.' SWAPO didn't have an office in Lusaka at the time. In fact, this was September 1964, just before Zambia gained full independence.

'OK,' Tuta said, 'I'll see what I can do. We've been invited to a UNIP† Conference in Mulungushi not far from Lusaka. Let's try to work out something.' We agreed to meet again later.

I had had no contact with any liberation movements while travelling through Angola, though I'd heard about them at home. In the Angola bush where I had travelled people didn't yet know much about the struggle in Angola. They had heard about Kaunda. Some even said, 'We know Kaunda, he will come to free us. He is a very strong man.' I said, 'No, it's not Kaunda who will liberate you. You the Angolan people must liberate yourselves.'

But they still had no idea what was going on . . . Mind you, they were always very friendly. It was difficult for me to communicate with them since I didn't understand their language. One of the Angolans in our group knew Oshikwanyama and acted as interpreter.

That evening I went to see Tuta's friend, Sam Shinyama, another UPA man. To my surprise, he spoke to me in Oshikwanyama. 'Don't be surprised,' he said, 'I went to Ongwediva Boys' School for several years.' I told him how I'd left Namibia and that I was a member of SWAPO. We spent a long time talking about Namibia,

---

* *Unio das Populacoes de Angola*, Angolan nationalist movement

† United National Independence Party, which led Zambia to independence

Angola and politics. He explained how we would get to the UNIP Conference. We would have to ride on a Winela lorry as far as the Zambezi River crossing. It would then be dark and easy to hide in the bush. Somebody would then pick us up in another lorry at a nearby village.

The following day we got in the Winela lorry, telling them we wanted to get work at Katima Mulilo. Tuta, Sam and I were in the same lorry. We travelled the whole day on a sandy road, not reaching the Zambezi until 9 p.m. Everybody got off to relieve themselves and stretch their legs; the drivers went for beer. We hid in the bush and waited. After some thirty minutes the drivers came back and the lorry took off with everybody but the three of us.

The nearby villagers gave us food and we slept there. Next day Tuta's brother-in-law came with a lorry and gave us a ride to Senanga. Tuta knew many people in the area — his wife was a Lozi from Senanga. We drove the whole day on a very bad road and arrived at Tuta's village in the evening. They gave us food and a place to sleep.

In Senanga I was introduced to William Mwanangombe, the local UNIP representative. I told him I was going to the UNIP Conference. He took a long look at me.

'You look in bad shape, brother! Don't you have any shoes?'

'I lost them in Namibia running away from the police,' I said.

He gave me a pair of his own, but they were very old and small. I had to cut off the backs in order to use them.

William, too, was going to the conference and promised to help me. 'Don't worry, brother, from now on UNIP will take care of you. We'll be leaving tomorrow.'

Early the next morning we all caught the bus for Mongu. We travelled legally this time and William got me on for free since I didn't have much money . . . ten shillings, hardly enough for food for a day or two. At Mongu we went to the UNIP office where some comrades were waiting with a Land Rover. We left for Broken Hill right away; a long ride, but the road wasn't as bad as before.

When the three-day conference ended I got a ride with some UNIP people to Lusaka. My plan was to cable SWAPO from there and ask for money so I could take the bus to Dar. First I went to the office in charge of refugees. A man named Cunningham was inside.

'Are you with SWAPO?' he asked.

'Yes.' I decided not to say more than I had to.

'Well, you're lucky! We have some other SWAPO people here and they've been waiting for travel money for two weeks. It came today so perhaps you'll be leaving with them tonight.'

The group was led by Joseph Helao Shityuwete. He had worked with me in Walvis Bay. When they came to the office, Cunningham asked if we knew each other.

'Oh yes,' Helao said, 'Ndadi is one of our leaders.'

'Very well, take him to Immigration and get him a travel pass to Mbeya.' Mbeya is on the Zambia-Tanganyika border.

At Immigration they fined me one pound for entering the country illegally. Helao paid it for me and I got my pass. Then we went to Kamwala bus station and picked up our tickets. At 8 p.m. we were on our way to Tanzania. I had been really lucky, getting out of Lusaka in less than a day.

At Mbeya, however, my luck turned. While waiting for the bus to Dar es Salaam, I was hit with a bad attack of malaria. I was taken to hospital where I spent two weeks. I've never been so sick in my life. I think that if I hadn't gone to hospital, I would have died.

I finally arrived in Dar es Salaam on 28 September 1964 and was given a warm welcome by comrades in the office.

Postscript

Tanzania was the first independent African country to open its doors for SWAPO to operate freely from its soil.

The opening of the SWAPO office in Dar es Salaam in 1963 coincided with the formation of the Organisation of African Unity (OAU). It was also the year SWAPO started training some of its cadres in guerrilla warfare in friendly countries. This led to SWAPO's immediate recognition by the OAU — having proved itself to be a serious liberation movement.

Since I had just arrived from home, the comrades I found in Dar es Salaam, Sam Nujoma, Peter Nanyemba and others, assigned me a duty of broadcasting directly to the Namibian people, using Radio Tanzania External transmitters, with other comrades using languages spoken in Namibia.

The SWAPO radio programme became very effective, politicising the people at home by informing them what SWAPO was doing outside and also inside the country. The Boers themselves were listening too, and decided to set up various FM radio stations all over Namibia to counter the SWAPO programme with lies and deception.

However, our people knew where the truth was coming from. When the enemy realised that our people were not interested in listening to their lies and cheap propaganda, they began to jam our programme but this became ineffective when we started broadcasting from Lusaka, Zambia. The racist police and their informers also noted those who frequently tuned into the SWAPO programmes. They started to threaten them and issued public warnings that anyone found listening to Radio Tanzania or Radio Zambia would be dealt with severely.

In June 1966 I was transferred to Cairo as SWAPO representative there. That was the time of Gamal Abdel Nasser in Egypt, while in

Namibia SWAPO had launched the armed struggle after the International Court of Justice had failed to rule against South Africa's occupation of our country.

In December 1971, growing political awareness amongst the contract workers of Namibia led to a general strike by 20,000 workers. The strikers returned to their homes in the north, and a generalised uprising took place in Ovamboland. Although the strike was broken, and the contract system remained, workers had showed their power and waves of strikes took place during the 1970s.

In March 1972, I was transferred from Cairo to Lusaka. As I had acquired knowledge in broadcasting, the SWAPO Executive assigned me to open up our radio programme there. We were offered some facilities at Zambia Broadcasting Services — not only SWAPO but other liberation movements as well, such as MPLA, FRELIMO, ZANU.

In 1974 Portuguese colonialism in Angola collapsed and many Namibians came to join SWAPO abroad. Those who had better educational backgrounds were assigned to broadcasting, and the problem of manpower became something of the past.

The following year the SWAPO Executive sent me to London to do a course in broadcasting journalism with the BBC. After training in London, I went to Finland, where I participated in a week of solidarity organised by Reverend Mikko Ihamaki, a Finnish missionary expelled from Namibia because of his involvement in politics. I addressed many meetings there, explaining to the Finnish people why it was necessary for the people of Namibia to take up arms and fight for their freedom and human dignity.

After my mission to Finland, I returned to Zambia and resumed my work at Zambia Broadcasting Services. But in 1976, at an enlarged Central Committee meeting I was appointed Director of the Voice of Namibia, as our radio was now called, in the Department of Information and Publicity.

When Angola attained independence in November 1975 the SWAPO Executive transferred me to Luanda, to open up a SWAPO radio programme there. We started broadcasting five months later; the station had to be re-organised to accommodate us.

While I was in Luanda, the South Africa regime ordered its paratroopers to attack a Namibian refugee settlement at Cassinga in southern Angola. The camp which was mostly used by people running away from Boer oppression in Namibia, was bombed with napalm and toxic gases. More than 700 Namibian men, women and children were cold-bloodedly murdered and hundreds more wounded or maimed.

I was at Cassinga shortly before it was destroyed, and met with a girl called Therezia, to whom I became engaged. Fortunately she was one of those who survived the massacre. We married the same year (1978), and we now have two boys, Jason Hamutenya Ndadi and Shitaleni Medondjo Ndadi.

I remained with the Department of Information and Publicity until 1983, when the Executive sent me to the German Democratic Republic for a 10-month course in political science.

When I returned to Luanda, I was appointed as SWAPO's representative to the Popular and Democratic Republic of Algeria.

Today, as I write, the blood of the Namibian men and women that has been shed during 22 years of armed liberation struggle is about to be crowned with victory. During 1988 the Boers were forced into negotiations after decisive battles at Cuito Cuanavale in southern Angola, where the SWAPO combatants fought side-by-side with Angolan and Cuban forces. Had the Boers not been defeated in Angola by our combined forces they would not have agreed to the negotiating table. They would have continued with their arrogant and intransigent attitude toward the people of Angola and Namibia's independence.

Having been in the liberation struggle right from the beginning, I know that if the people of Namibia, under the leadership of SWAPO and our president Sam Nujoma, had not taken up arms to fight for freedom, Namibia would have been a colony of racist South Africa for many more years to come.

Algiers, January 1989

Glossary: acronyms and terms as used in this book

African	original inhabitants of Namibia
baas	boss or employer
Black	alternative term for African
Boer	White South African/Afrikaner
Coloured	applied to people deemed to be mixed in terms of apartheid population classification
compound	housing complex or barracks, usually fenced off
contract	terms under which migrant workers were compelled to work
ertjies	peas
European	alternative term for White
IP	Identification Pass
Kaffir	insulting term for African
kataula	narrow-guage railway
knobkierie	stick
kraal	homestead
location	urban residential area
mealie	maize
missus	wife of *baas*, or female boss or employer
Native Affairs	South African state department responsible for administration of Africans
OPC	Ovamboland People's Congress, formed in Cape Town in 1957, precursor of OPO
OPO	Ovamboland People's Organisation, precurser of SWAPO in Namibia
olupale	reception/sitting room in traditional homestead
omakatana	machete
oshifima	thick porridge
oshikundu	maize or millet porridge
oshinghumbi	best man or bridesmaid
oubaas	old boss or employer
Oukwanyama	One of the seven areas now making up Ovamboland, hence Oshikwanyama, the language spoken there and Ovakwanyama, the people
Ovamboland	central area of northern Namibia

pap	porridge
pondok	contract workers' accommodation
Police Zone	area of colonial settlement and policing in Namibia — the north was unpoliced
South West Africa	South African name for Namibia
SWANLA	South West Africa Native Labour Association, labour recruiting agency
SWAPO	South West African People's Organisation, Namibia's liberation movement
UNIP	United National Independence Party of Zambia
UPA	*Unio das Populacoes de Angola*, Angolan nationalist movement
White	colonial and settler minority in Namibia
Winela	Witwatersrand Native Labour Association, South African mine-labour recruiting agency

INTERNATIONAL DEFENCE AND AID FUND FOR SOUTHERN AFRICA
Canon Collins House, 64 Essex Road, London N1 8LR

The specific mandate of IDAF is to ensure the legal defence of the victims of apart-
~id, to aid their families and dependants, and to inform the world about apartheid
~d the struggle against it.

~ere can be no real peace in Southern Africa until the peoples of Namibia and South
~rica have been liberated. South Africa attacks neighbouring states causing wide-
~read destruction and suffering. Opponents of apartheid living abroad have become
~rgets for assassinations and massacres.

~outh Africa and Namibia, the heightened repression has placed increasing
~mands on the work of IDAF. Behind a curtain of censorship and legislation, the
~als and imprisonment, the detention and torture, the forced removals and
~nnings, the violence and killings go on remorselessly, at a more terrible level than
~er before.

~ very special concern for IDAF is the children, who have been made the particular target of the apartheid
~gime, and face a calculated and brutal onslaught from its armed forces and police.

~e urgently need your support. Make your contribution to a free, just and peaceful Southern Africa. Send your
~nation, large or small, to our Fund at its Head Office at the address above, or to one of the addresses below."

$+$ Trevor Huddleston (B).

Archbishop Trevor Huddleston, Chair of the Trustees of IDAF

~e International Defence and Aid Fund for Southern Africa is a humanitarian organisation founded by Canon
~John Collins, dedicated to the achievement of free, democratic, non-racial societies in South Africa and
~mibia.

~e International Defence and Aid Fund for Southern Africa is associated with a registered English charity, the
~l Plaatje Educational Project Limited, which assists with the education of children who are victims of apart-
~d.

~AF has National Committees in various countries. Their accounts are audited and they are part of the Fund.
~r convenience supporters may wish to send contributions to them at the following addresses: please address
~ur donation to Archbishop Trevor Huddleston.

~NADA
AFSA-Canada
~4 Albert St #200
~tawa, K1P 6E6
~l: (613)-233-5939

~ELAND
AFSA-Ireland
~ Box 1974
~blin 18
~l: (01) 895035

~THERLANDS
~F-Nederland
~omme Nieuwegracht 10
~2 HG Utrecht
~: (30) 313194
~stgiro a/c no. 2989732-Hilversum

~W ZEALAND
~DAF
~ Box 17303
~rori
~llington 5

NORWAY
IDAF-Norway
PO Box 2
Lindeberg Gaard
N-1007 Oslo 10
Tel: (2) 301345
Postgiro a/c no: 2616670

SWEDEN
International Defence and Aid Fund (IDAF)
c/o Lennart Renöfelt,
Månskensgatan 34F,
S-80274 GÄVLE
Postgiro a/c no: 4093290-7

UNITED KINGDOM
BDAFSA
22 The Ivories
6–8 Northampton Street
London N1 2HX
Tel: (01) 354 1462
Postgiro a/c no: 5 11 7151

UNITED STATES OF AMERICA
IDAFSA-US
PO Box 17
Cambridge, Ma 02138
Tel: (617) 491 8343

OTHER TITLES IN THE CLASSIC REPRINT SERIES

THE RISE OF THE SOUTH AFRICAN REICH

Brian Bunting

One of the most readable and re-vealing analyses of the origins and development of the apartheid regime. The reprint takes the place of the original edition published by the Penguin African Library in 1964 and revised in 1969.

1986 £6.00 paperback. $8\frac{1}{4} \times 5\frac{3}{4}''$ 552pp. ISBN 0 904759 74 1 Book No. DO97
1986 £12.00 hardback $8\frac{1}{2} \times 6''$ 552pp. ISBN 0 904759 75 X Book No. DO971

SOUTH AFRICA THE STRUGGLE FOR A BIRTHRIGHT

Mary Benson

South Africa — The Struggle For A Birthright is a classic account of the African National Congress from its beginnings in 1912 up until 1965. It is not, however, a dry rendering of historical facts. The author knew and interviewed personally many of the leading figures in the ANC, and by blending their stories into the overall picture has produced a unique document of social, historical and political significance.

This reprint, with a new preface by the author, takes the place of the original edition published by the Penguin African Library in 1966.

1985 £4.00 Paperback $8\frac{1}{4} \times 5\frac{3}{4}''$ 314pp. ISBN 0 904759 67 9 Book No. DO90
1985 £8.00 Hardback $8\frac{1}{2} \times 6''$ 314pp. ISBN 0 904759 68 7 Book No. DO901

SOUTH AFRICA THE PEASANTS' REVOLT

Govan Mbeki

The Transkei was the first bantu-stan created by the apartheid regime; this book focuses on developments in the Transkei when resistance to the imposition of the bantustan took the form of open rebellion.

Govan Mbeki, a leading member of the African National Congress, was released from Robben Island in November 1987 after serving 23 years of his sentence of life imprisonment.

This reprint takes the place of the original edition published by the Penguin African Library in 1964.

1984 £3.00 Paperback $8\frac{1}{4} \times 5\frac{3}{4}''$ 160pp. ISBN 0 904759 57 1 Book No. DO83

CLASS AND COLOUR IN SOUTH AFRICA 1850–1950

Jack and Ray Simons

As a critical analysis of the Labour and National Movements in South Africa, *Class and Colour* has become essential reading for those engaged in the struggle for South African libera-tion. It is also an invaluable book for students of race relations, colonial nationalism, class theory and South African history.

This reprint takes the place of the original edition published by the Penguin African Library in 1969.

1983 £7.50 $8\frac{1}{4} \times 5\frac{3}{4}''$ 702pp. ISBN 0 904759 52 0 Book No. DO75
1983 £15.00 $8\frac{1}{2} \times 6''$ 702pp. ISBN 0 904759 52 0 Book No. DO751.

For further details of this series or for a copy of the International Defence & Aid Fund for Southern Africa catalogue, please write to IDAF Publications Ltd., Canon Collins House, 64 Essex Road, London N1 8LR